FAVORITE BRAND NAME

One-Dish Recipes

Publications International, Ltd.

Favorite Brand Name Recipes at www.fbnr.com

Pictured on the front cover: Ravioli with Homemade Tomato Sauce *(page 352)*.
Pictured on the back cover *(clockwise from left):* Hearty Potato and Sausage Bake *(page 30)*, Chili with Beans and Corn *(page 324)* and Spicy Tuna and Linguine with Garlic and Pine Nuts *(page 160)*.

ISBN: 0-7853-7997-5

Library of Congress Control Number: 2002117339

Manufactured in China.

8 7 6 5 4 3 2 1

Nutritional Analysis: The nutritional information that appears with some recipes was submitted in part by the participating companies and associations. Every effort has been made to check the accuracy of these numbers. However, because numerous variables account for a wide range of values for certain foods, nutritive analyses in this book should be considered approximate.

Microwave Cooking: Microwave ovens vary in wattage. Use the cooking times as guidelines and check for doneness before adding more time.

Preparation/Cooking Times: Preparation times are based on the approximate amount of time required to assemble the recipe before cooking, baking, chilling or serving. These times include preparation steps such as measuring, chopping and mixing. The fact that some preparations and cooking can be done simultaneously is taken into account. Preparation of optional ingredients and serving suggestions is not included.

Contents

pg. 30

pg. 162

pg. 308

A hearty meal all in

one casserole dish

means less time

preparing and

cleaning up. So get

out of the kitchen

and let your oven do

the work for you.

Velveeta® Spicy Chicken Spaghetti

12 ounces spaghetti, uncooked
4 boneless skinless chicken breast halves (about 1¼ pounds), cut into strips
1 pound (16 ounces) VELVEETA® Pasteurized Prepared Cheese Product, cut up
1 can (10¾ ounces) condensed cream of chicken soup
1 can (10 ounces) diced tomatoes and green chilies, undrained
1 can (4½ ounces) sliced mushrooms, drained
⅓ cup milk

1. Cook pasta as directed on package; drain. Return to same pan.

2. Spray skillet with no stick cooking spray. Add chicken; cook and stir on medium-high heat 4 to 5 minutes or until cooked through. Add Velveeta, soup, tomatoes and green chilies, mushrooms and milk; stir on low heat until Velveeta is melted. Add chicken mixture to pasta; toss to coat. Spoon into greased 13×9-inch baking dish.

3. Bake at 350°F for 35 to 40 minutes or until hot.   *Makes 6 to 8 servings*

Prep Time: 5 minutes
Bake Time: 40 minutes

Velveeta® Spicy Chicken Spaghetti

Chicken Enchiladas

 1 whole chicken (about 3 pounds), cut into 8 pieces
 3 fresh poblano chilies, roasted, peeled, seeded, deveined and diced
 1 large tomato, peeled, seeded and chopped
 ½ cup finely chopped white onion
 1 clove garlic, minced
 ½ teaspoon ground cumin
 ¼ teaspoon salt
 ½ cup chicken broth
 1½ cups heavy cream
 12 corn tortillas (6-inch diameter)
 2 cups (8 ounces) shredded queso Chihuahua or Monterey Jack cheese
   Green onions and slivered red bell peppers for garnish

1. Place chicken in single layer in 12-inch skillet. Sprinkle with chilies, tomato, white onion, garlic, cumin and salt; add broth. Bring to a boil over medium-high heat. Reduce heat. Cover; simmer 1 hour or until chicken is tender.

2. Remove chicken from skillet with tongs, shaking off vegetable pieces. Let stand until cool enough to handle.

3. Skim and discard fat from skillet. Bring remaining broth mixture to a boil over medium-high heat. Boil 4 to 8 minutes until mixture is reduced to 2 cups. Pour reduced broth mixture into 13×9-inch baking dish.

4. Remove and discard skin and bones from chicken. Using fingers, pull chicken into coarse shreds.

5. Preheat oven to 375°F. Heat cream in medium skillet over medium heat to just below boiling; remove from heat.

6. Dip 1 tortilla in cream with tongs a few seconds or until limp. Remove, draining off excess cream. Spread about 3 tablespoons chicken down center of tortilla.

7. Roll up; place on sauce in baking dish. Repeat with remaining tortillas, cream and chicken. Pour any remaining cream over enchiladas.

8. Sprinkle cheese over enchiladas. Bake 25 to 30 minutes until sauce is bubbly and cheese is melted. Garnish, if desired.   *Makes 4 to 6 servings*

6

Chicken Enchiladas

Chicken Caesar Tetrazzini

8 ounces uncooked spaghetti
2 cups shredded or cubed cooked chicken
1 cup chicken broth
1 cup HIDDEN VALLEY® Caesar Dressing
1 jar (4½ ounces) sliced mushrooms, drained
½ cup grated Parmesan cheese
2 tablespoons dry bread crumbs

Cook spaghetti according to package directions. Drain and combine with chicken, broth, dressing and mushrooms in a large mixing bowl. Place mixture in a 2-quart casserole. Mix together cheese and bread crumbs; sprinkle over spaghetti mixture. Bake at 350°F. for 25 minutes or until casserole is hot and bubbly.　　　　　*Makes 4 servings*

Turkey Broccoli Bake

1 bag (16 ounces) frozen broccoli cuts, thawed, drained
2 cups cubed cooked turkey or chicken
2 cups soft bread cubes
8 ounces sliced American cheese, divided
1 jar (12 ounces) HEINZ® HomeStyle Turkey or Chicken Gravy
½ cup undiluted evaporated milk
　Dash pepper

In buttered 9-inch square baking dish, layer broccoli, turkey, bread cubes and cheese. Combine gravy, milk and pepper; pour over cheese. Bake in 375°F oven, 40 minutes. Let stand 5 minutes before serving.　　　　　*Makes 6 servings*

8

Chicken Caesar Tetrazzini

Fast 'n' Fancy Casserole

1 package (10 ounces) PERDUE® SHORT CUTS® Fresh Original Roasted Carved Chicken Breast
1 package (8 to 10 ounces) frozen peas and carrots
1 jar (17 ounces) Alfredo sauce
6 ounces (1½ cups uncooked) fusilli, rotelle or ziti, cooked and drained
1 package (8 ounces) shredded Italian cheeses with seasonings (2 cups), divided
Salt and ground pepper to taste

Preheat oven to 375°F. Grease 8- to 9-inch square baking dish. In medium bowl, combine chicken, vegetables, sauce, pasta and 1 cup cheese. Season with salt and pepper; mix well. Top with remaining cheese. Bake 20 minutes or until bubbly. *Makes 4 servings*

Prep Time: 5 to 10 minutes
Cook Time: 20 minutes

10

Herbed Chicken and Potatoes

2 medium all-purpose potatoes, thinly sliced (about 1 pound)
4 bone-in chicken breast halves (about 2 pounds)*
1 envelope LIPTON® RECIPE SECRETS® Savory Herb with Garlic Soup Mix
⅓ cup water
1 tablespoon olive or vegetable oil

*Substitution: Use 1 (2½- to 3-pound) chicken; cut into serving pieces.

1. Preheat oven to 425°F. In 13×9-inch baking or roasting pan, add potatoes; arrange chicken over potatoes.

2. Pour soup mix blended with water and oil over chicken and potatoes.

3. Bake uncovered 40 minutes or until chicken is no longer pink in center and potatoes are tender. *Makes 4 servings*

Spicy Chicken Tortilla Casserole

 1 tablespoon vegetable oil
 1 cup chopped green bell pepper
 1 small onion, chopped
 2 cloves garlic, finely chopped
 1 pound (about 4) boneless, skinless chicken breast halves, cut into bite-size pieces
 1 jar (16 ounces) ORTEGA® SALSA (any flavor)
 1 can (2¼ ounces) sliced ripe olives
 6 corn tortillas, cut into halves
 2 cups (8 ounces) shredded Monterey Jack or Cheddar cheese
   Sour cream (optional)

PREHEAT oven to 350°F.

HEAT oil in large skillet over medium-high heat. Add bell pepper, onion and garlic; cook for 2 to 3 minutes or until vegetables are tender.

ADD chicken; cook, stirring frequently, for 3 to 5 minutes or until chicken is no longer pink in center. Stir in salsa and olives; remove from heat.

PLACE 6 tortilla halves onto bottom of ungreased 8-inch-square baking pan. Top with half of chicken mixture and 1 cup cheese; repeat.

BAKE for 15 to 20 minutes or until bubbly. Serve with sour cream.   *Makes 8 servings*

11

It is estimated that Americans consume about 1 billion pounds of tortillas every year. That is one tortilla per person every day.

Mexican Lasagna

4 boneless skinless chicken breast halves
2 tablespoons vegetable oil
2 teaspoons chili powder
1 teaspoon ground cumin
1 can (14½ ounces) diced tomatoes with garlic, drained
1 can (8 ounces) tomato sauce
1 teaspoon hot pepper sauce (optional)
1 cup part-skim ricotta cheese
1 can (4 ounces) diced green chilies
¼ cup chopped fresh cilantro, divided
12 (6-inch) corn tortillas
1 cup (4 ounces) shredded Cheddar cheese

Preheat oven to 375°F. Cut chicken into ½-inch pieces.

Heat oil in large skillet over medium heat. Add chicken, chili powder and cumin. Cook 4 minutes or until chicken is tender, stirring occasionally. Stir in diced tomatoes, tomato sauce and hot pepper sauce, if desired; bring to a boil. Reduce heat; simmer 2 minutes.

Combine ricotta cheese, chilies and 2 tablespoons cilantro in small bowl; mix until well blended.

Spoon half of chicken mixture into 12×8-inch baking dish. Top with 6 tortillas, ricotta cheese mixture, remaining 6 tortillas, remaining chicken mixture, Cheddar cheese and remaining 2 tablespoons cilantro. Bake 25 minutes or until heated through.   *Makes 6 to 8 servings*

Choose mild green chilies for this recipe. If diced tomatoes with garlic are not available, you may add one clove minced garlic to a can of diced tomatoes.

Mexican Lasagna

Zesty Turkey Pot Pie

1 tablespoon vegetable oil
1 small onion, finely chopped
1 jalapeño pepper,* seeded and minced
1 pound ground turkey
1 package (16 ounces) frozen mixed vegetables
½ teaspoon dried thyme leaves
½ teaspoon black pepper
2 cans (10¾ ounces each) golden mushroom soup
1 package (11 ounces) refrigerated breadsticks (12 breadsticks)

*Jalapeño peppers can sting and irritate the skin; wear rubber gloves when handling peppers and do not touch eyes. Wash hands after handling peppers.

1. Preheat oven to 350°F.

2. Heat oil in large skillet over medium heat. Add onion and jalapeño pepper; cook and stir 5 minutes or until tender. Add turkey; cook and stir until no longer pink, stirring to separate meat. Stir in vegetables, thyme and pepper. Cook 5 minutes until vegetables are thawed. Stir in soup. Cook 5 minutes or until heated through.

3. Spoon turkey mixture into greased 13×9-inch casserole. Pull and stretch breadsticks to lengthen, pressing ends together if necessary to reach across baking dish. Arrange breadsticks in lattice pattern over turkey, trimming ends. Bake 15 to 20 minutes or until breadsticks are golden. *Makes 6 servings*

Note: Mixture must be hot when spooned into casserole or breadsticks will become gummy on the bottom.

14

Zesty Turkey Pot Pie

Chicken Normandy Style

2 tablespoons butter, divided
3 cups peeled, thinly sliced apples (about 3 apples)
1 pound ground chicken
¼ cup apple brandy or apple juice
1 can (10¾ ounces) cream of chicken soup
¼ cup finely chopped green onions, green part only
2 teaspoons fresh minced sage *or* ½ teaspoon dried sage leaves
¼ teaspoon pepper
1 package (12 ounces) egg noodles, cooked and drained

1. Preheat oven to 350°F.

2. Melt 1 tablespoon butter in 12-inch nonstick skillet. Add apple slices; cook and stir over medium heat 7 to 10 minutes or until tender. Remove apple slices from skillet.

3. Add ground chicken to same skillet; cook and stir over medium heat until brown, breaking up with spoon. Stir in apple brandy and cook 2 minutes. Stir in soup, green onions, sage, pepper and apple slices. Simmer 5 minutes.

4. Toss noodles with remaining 1 tablespoon butter. Spoon into well-greased 9-inch square pan. Top with chicken mixture. Bake for 15 minutes or until hot.   *Makes 4 servings*

Note: Ground turkey, ground pork or tofu crumbles may be substituted for the ground chicken, if desired.

For this recipe choose apples that have a sweet rather than a tart flavor. Fugi and Braeburn apples work well.

16

Tuscan Noodle Bake

½ pound Italian sausage, casings removed and sausage crumbled
½ pound BUTTERBALL® Ground Turkey
1 cup chopped onion
1 teaspoon fresh minced garlic
1 can (15 ounces) HUNT'S® Tomato Sauce
1 can (14.5 ounces) HUNT'S® Whole Tomatoes, undrained and crushed
1 can (6 ounces) sliced mushrooms, drained
1 can (2¼ ounces) sliced black olives, drained
¼ cup chopped fresh parsley
1 teaspoon dried basil leaves
1 teaspoon dried oregano leaves
¼ teaspoon pepper
¼ cup TREASURE CAVE® Shredded Parmesan Cheese
½ package (12 ounces) wide egg noodles, cooked and drained
1 cup shredded mozzarella cheese

18

In large Dutch oven, brown sausage and turkey with onion and garlic until meat is no longer pink; drain. Add remaining ingredients except Parmesan cheese, noodles and mozzarella cheese; simmer 5 minutes. Stir in Parmesan cheese and noodles; blend well. Pour noodle mixture into greased 13×9×2-inch baking dish. Bake, covered, at 350°F for 20 minutes. Sprinkle mozzarella cheese over noodle mixture and bake, uncovered, for an additional 5 to 7 minutes.   *Makes 6 to 8 servings*

Chicken Parmesan Noodle Bake

1 package (12 ounces) extra-wide noodles
4 boneless, skinless chicken breast halves
¼ teaspoon rosemary, crushed
2 cans (14½ ounces each) DEL MONTE® Diced Tomatoes with Basil, Garlic & Oregano
½ cup (2 ounces) shredded mozzarella cheese
¼ cup (1 ounce) grated Parmesan cheese

1. Preheat oven to 450°F.

2. Cook noodles according to package directions; drain.

3. Meanwhile, sprinkle chicken with rosemary; season with salt and pepper, if desired. Arrange chicken in 13×9-inch baking dish. Bake, uncovered, 20 minutes or until chicken is no longer pink in center. Drain; remove chicken from dish.

4. Drain tomatoes, reserving liquid. In large bowl, toss reserved liquid with noodles; place in baking dish. Top with chicken and tomatoes; sprinkle with cheeses.

5. Bake 10 minutes or until heated through. Sprinkle with additional Parmesan cheese and garnish, if desired.   *Makes 4 servings*

Prep & Cook Time: 35 minutes

Chicken Tetrazzini

   8 ounces uncooked spaghetti, broken in half
   3 tablespoons butter, divided
   ¼ cup all-purpose flour
   1 teaspoon salt
   ½ teaspoon paprika
   ½ teaspoon celery salt
   ⅛ teaspoon pepper
   2 cups milk
   1 cup chicken broth
   3 cups chopped cooked chicken
   1 can (4 ounces) mushrooms, drained
   ¼ cup pimiento strips
   ¾ cup (3 ounces) grated Wisconsin Parmesan cheese, divided

In large saucepan, cook spaghetti according to package directions; drain. Return to same saucepan; add 1 tablespoon butter. Stir until melted. Set aside. In 3-quart saucepan, melt remaining 2 tablespoons butter over medium heat; stir in flour, salt, paprika, celery salt and pepper. Remove from heat; gradually stir in milk and chicken broth. Cook over medium heat, stirring constantly, until thickened. Add chicken, mushrooms, pimiento, spaghetti and ¼ cup cheese; heat thoroughly. Place chicken mixture on ovenproof platter or in shallow casserole; sprinkle remaining ½ cup cheese over top. Broil about 3 inches from heat until lightly browned.   *Makes 6 to 8 servings*

Favorite recipe from **Wisconsin Milk Marketing Board**

19

Chicken 'n' Rice Filled Cabbage Rolls

12 large whole green cabbage leaves
¾ medium onion, chopped
1 clove garlic, minced
1 tablespoon vegetable oil
1 can (15 ounces) tomato sauce
½ cup water
3 tablespoons packed light brown sugar
3 tablespoons lemon juice
⅛ teaspoon ground allspice
3 cups finely chopped cooked chicken
1 cup cooked rice, cooled
1 egg, beaten
¾ teaspoon salt
⅛ teaspoon black pepper

20

Bring 6 cups water to a boil in Dutch oven over high heat. Add cabbage leaves and reduce heat to low. Simmer, covered, 10 to 12 minutes or until cabbage leaves are tender. Drain; rinse under cold running water.

Cook and stir onion and garlic in oil in large skillet over medium heat 6 to 8 minutes or until tender. Remove ½ cup onion mixture. Add tomato sauce, ½ cup water, brown sugar, lemon juice and allspice to onion mixture in skillet. Cook, uncovered, 10 minutes, stirring occasionally.

Combine reserved onion mixture, chicken, rice, egg, salt and black pepper; mix well. Place about ⅓ cup mixture in center of each cabbage leaf. Fold sides over filling; roll up.

Preheat oven to 350°F. Spread ½ cup tomato sauce over bottom of 13×9-inch baking dish. Arrange cabbage rolls, seam side down, over sauce. Spoon remaining sauce evenly over cabbage rolls; cover with foil. Bake 1 hour and 15 minutes or until very tender.

Makes 4 to 6 servings

Chicken 'n' Rice Filled Cabbage Rolls

Moroccan Chicken, Apricot & Almond Casserole

1 pound ground chicken*
¾ teaspoon salt, divided
¼ teaspoon ground cinnamon
¼ teaspoon black pepper
1 tablespoon olive oil
1 small onion, peeled and chopped
1 cup sliced dried apricots
½ teaspoon red pepper flakes
½ teaspoon ground ginger
1 can (28 ounces) diced tomatoes, undrained
1 can (10¾ ounces) chicken broth
½ cup water
1 cup large-pearl couscous**
¼ cup sliced almonds, toasted

*Ground turkey or lamb may be substituted for the ground chicken, if desired.

**Large-pearl couscous, which is the size of barley, is available in many supermarkets. If it is not available, substitute regular small-grain couscous.

1. Preheat oven to 325°F.

2. Combine ground chicken, ½ teaspoon salt, cinnamon and black pepper in medium bowl. Shape into 1-inch balls. Heat oil in large skillet. Add chicken and brown on all sides. Remove to a plate. Add onion and apricots to skillet. Cook mixture 5 minutes over medium heat or until onion is tender. Stir in remaining ¼ teaspoon salt, red pepper flakes, ginger and tomatoes with juice. Simmer 5 minutes.

3. Meanwhile, bring chicken broth and water to a boil in small saucepan. Stir in large-pearl couscous.*** Reduce heat; cover and simmer 10 minutes or until couscous is tender and almost all liquid has is absorbed. Drain if necessary.

4. Spoon couscous into greased 11×7-inch casserole dish. Top with chicken and spoon on tomato mixture. Bake 20 minutes or until chicken is no longer pink in center. Sprinkle with almonds.   *Makes 4 to 6 servings*

***To cook small-grain couscous follow package directions using 1 cup chicken broth in place of water. Remove from heat and let stand 5 minutes or until all liquid is absorbed. Fluff with a fork.

Moroccan Chicken, Apricot &
Almond Casserole

Zesty Italian Stuffed Peppers

    3 bell peppers (green, red or yellow), cut in half lengthwise, seeds discarded
    1 pound ground beef
    1 jar (14 ounces) spaghetti sauce
 1⅓ cups *French's®* French Fried Onions, divided
    2 tablespoons *Frank's® RedHot®* Cayenne Pepper Sauce
    ½ cup uncooked instant rice
    ¼ cup sliced ripe olives
    1 cup (4 ounces) shredded mozzarella cheese

Preheat oven to 400°F. Place peppers, cut side up, in shallow 2-quart baking dish; set aside.

Place beef in large microwavable bowl. Microwave on HIGH 5 minutes or until meat is browned, stirring once. Drain. Stir in spaghetti sauce, ⅔ *cup* French Fried Onions, **Frank's RedHot** Sauce, rice and olives. Spoon evenly into bell pepper halves.

Cover; bake 35 minutes or until bell peppers are tender. Uncover; sprinkle with cheese and remaining ⅔ *cup* onions. Bake 1 minute or until onions are golden.   *Makes 6 servings*

Prep Time: 10 minutes
Cook Time: 36 minutes

24

Monterey Black Bean Tortilla Supper

    1 pound ground beef, browned and drained
 1½ cups bottled salsa
    1 (15-ounce) can black beans, drained
    4 (8-inch) flour tortillas
    2 cups (8 ounces) shredded Wisconsin Monterey Jack cheese*

*For authentic Mexican flavor, substitute 2 cups shredded Wisconsin Queso Blanco.

Heat oven to 400°F. Combine ground beef, salsa and beans. In lightly greased 2-quart round casserole, layer one tortilla, ⅔ cup meat mixture and ½ cup cheese. Repeat layers three times. Bake 30 minutes or until heated through.   *Makes 5 to 6 servings*

*Favorite recipe from **Wisconsin Milk Marketing Board***

Zesty Italian Stuffed Pepper

Spaghetti Bake

1 pound BOB EVANS® Dinner Link Sausage (regular or Italian)
1 (8-ounce) can tomato sauce
1 (6-ounce) can tomato paste
1 (4-ounce) can sliced mushrooms, drained
½ teaspoon salt
½ teaspoon dried basil leaves
½ teaspoon dried oregano leaves
6 ounces spaghetti, cooked according to package directions and drained
⅓ cup shredded mozzarella cheese
2 tablespoons grated Parmesan cheese
Fresh basil leaves and tomato slices (optional)

Preheat oven to 375°F. Cut sausage links into bite-size pieces. Cook in medium skillet over medium heat until browned, stirring occasionally. Drain off any drippings; set aside. Combine tomato sauce, tomato paste, mushrooms, salt, dried basil and oregano in large bowl. Add spaghetti and reserved sausage; mix well. Spoon into lightly greased 1½-quart casserole dish; sprinkle with cheeses. Bake 20 to 30 minutes or until heated through. Garnish with fresh basil and tomato slices, if desired. Serve hot. Refrigerate leftovers.   *Makes 4 servings*

Italian sausage, which is a good choice for this casserole, owes its distinctive sweet licoricelike flavor to fennel seeds or anise seeds. It is available in both hot and mild varieties.

26

Spaghetti Bake

Pork Chops and Apple Stuffing Bake

6 (¾-inch-thick) boneless pork loin chops (about 1½ pounds)
¼ teaspoon salt
⅛ teaspoon black pepper
1 tablespoon vegetable oil
1 small onion, chopped
2 ribs celery, chopped
2 Granny Smith apples, peeled, cored and coarsely chopped (about 2 cups)
1 can (14½ ounces) reduced-sodium chicken broth
1 can (10¾ ounces) condensed cream of celery soup, undiluted
¼ cup dry white wine
6 cups herb-seasoned stuffing cubes

Preheat oven to 375°F. Spray 13×9-inch baking dish with nonstick cooking spray.

Season both sides of pork chops with salt and pepper. Heat oil in large deep skillet over medium-high heat until hot. Add chops and cook until browned on both sides, turning once. Remove chops from skillet; set aside.

Add onion and celery to same skillet. Cook and stir 3 minutes or until onion is tender. Add apples; cook and stir 1 minute. Add broth, soup and wine; mix well. Bring to a simmer; remove from heat. Stir in stuffing cubes until evenly moistened.

Spread stuffing mixture evenly in prepared dish. Place pork chops on top of stuffing; pour any accumulated juices over chops.

Cover tightly with foil and bake 30 to 40 minutes or until pork chops are juicy and barely pink in center.   *Makes 6 servings*

Pork Chop and Apple Stuffing Bake

Hearty Potato and Sausage Bake

1 pound new potatoes, cut in halves or quarters
1 large onion, sliced
½ pound baby carrots
2 tablespoons butter, melted
1 teaspoon salt
1 teaspoon garlic powder
½ teaspoon dried thyme leaves
½ teaspoon black pepper
1 pound cooked chicken sausage or turkey sausage

Preheat oven to 400°F. Spray 13×9-inch baking pan with nonstick cooking spray.

Combine potatoes, onion, carrots, butter, salt, garlic powder, thyme and pepper in large bowl. Toss to coat evenly.

Place potato mixture into prepared pan; bake, uncovered, 30 minutes. Add sausage to potato mixture; mix well. Continue to bake 15 to 20 minutes or until potatoes are tender and golden brown.

Makes 4 to 6 servings

New potatoes are small young potatoes. They may be any variety, but most often they are round red potatoes. Their sugar content has not been completely converted to starch so they have a crisp, waxy texture.

Hearty Potato and Sausage Bake

Baked Pasta with Beef and Beans

¼ cup CRISCO® Oil,* divided
½ pound uncooked mostaccioli or penne pasta
1 pound ground beef *or* ½ pound ground beef and ½ pound Italian sausage
1 small onion, peeled and chopped
2 teaspoons jarred minced garlic *or* 1 large garlic clove, peeled and minced
1 can (14½ ounces) chopped tomatoes, drained
1 tablespoon tomato paste
1 teaspoon Italian seasoning
½ teaspoon salt
¼ teaspoon freshly ground black pepper
1 can (8 ounces) kidney beans, drained and rinsed
¼ cup freshly grated Parmesan cheese
1 cup (4 ounces) shredded mozzarella or provolone cheese

*Use your favorite Crisco Oil product.

32

1. Heat oven to 400°F.

2. Bring large pot of salted water to a boil. Add 2 tablespoons oil and pasta. Cook pasta according to package directions until al dente. Drain.

3. While pasta is cooking, heat large skillet on medium-high heat. Add beef. Cook 3 minutes, breaking up with fork, or until no longer pink. Remove from pan. Discard drippings. Wipe out skillet.

4. Heat remaining 2 tablespoons oil in skillet on medium-high heat. Add onion and garlic. Cook 3 minutes, or until onion is translucent. Return beef to pan. Add tomatoes, tomato paste, Italian seasoning, salt and pepper. Stir well. Cook 5 minutes.

5. Combine pasta, meat mixture and beans in 13×9×2-inch baking dish. Sprinkle with cheeses. Bake at 400°F for 20 to 30 minutes, or until cheese is melted. Serve immediately.

Makes 4 servings

Note: The dish can be prepared a day in advance of baking and refrigerated, tightly covered with plastic wrap. If chilled, bake at 375°F for 35 to 45 minutes.

Preparation Time: 30 minutes
Total Time: 50 to 60 minutes

Southwest Ham 'n Cheese Quiche

   4 (8-inch) flour tortillas
   2 tablespoons butter or margarine, melted
   2 cups pizza 4-cheese blend
1½ cups (8 ounces) diced CURE 81® ham
   ½ cup sour cream
   ¼ cup salsa
   3 eggs, beaten
     Salsa
     Sour cream

Heat oven to 350°F. Cut 3 tortillas in half. Place remaining whole tortilla in bottom of greased 10-inch quiche dish or tart pan; brush with melted butter. Arrange tortilla halves around edge of dish, rounded sides up, overlapping to form pastry shell. Brush with remaining butter. Place 9-inch round cake pan inside quiche dish. Bake 5 minutes. Cool; remove cake pan. In bowl, combine cheese and ham. Stir in ½ cup sour cream, ¼ cup salsa and eggs. Pour into tortilla shell. Bake 55 to 60 minutes or until knife inserted in center comes out clean. Let stand 5 minutes. Serve with additional salsa and sour cream. *Makes 6 servings*

33

Sausage and Polenta Casserole

   1 tablespoon olive oil
   1 cup chopped mushrooms
   1 small red bell pepper, cored, seeded and diced
   1 small onion, diced
   1 pound hot or mild bulk Italian sausage
   1 jar (28 to 30 ounces) meatless pasta sauce
   1 roll (16 to 18 ounces) polenta

1. Preheat oven to 350°F.

2. Heat oil in large skillet. Add mushrooms, bell pepper and onion; cook and stir over medium heat 5 minutes or until tender. Add sausage; cook and stir until sausage is brown, breaking into small pieces with spoon. Drain. Stir in pasta sauce and simmer 5 minutes.

3. Cut polenta roll into 9 slices and arrange in greased 9-inch square casserole. Top with sausage mixture. Bake for 15 minutes or until heated through. *Makes 4 servings*

Lasagna Supreme

8 ounces uncooked lasagna noodles
½ pound ground beef
½ pound mild Italian sausage, casings removed
1 medium onion, chopped
2 cloves garlic, minced
1 can (14½ ounces) whole peeled tomatoes, undrained and chopped
1 can (6 ounces) tomato paste
2 teaspoons dried basil leaves
1 teaspoon dried marjoram leaves
1 can (4 ounces) sliced mushrooms, drained
2 eggs
2 cups (16 ounces) cream-style cottage cheese
¾ cup grated Parmesan cheese, divided
2 tablespoons dried parsley flakes
½ teaspoon salt
½ teaspoon black pepper
2 cups (8 ounces) shredded Cheddar cheese
3 cups (12 ounces) shredded mozzarella cheese

1. Cook lasagna noodles according to package directions; drain.

2. Cook meats, onion and garlic in large skillet over medium-high heat until meat is brown, stirring to separate meat. Drain drippings from skillet.

3. Add tomatoes with juice, tomato paste, basil and marjoram. Reduce heat to low. Cover; simmer 15 minutes, stirring often. Stir in mushrooms; set aside.

4. Preheat oven to 375°F. Beat eggs in large bowl; add cottage cheese, ½ cup Parmesan cheese, parsley, salt and pepper. Mix well.

5. Place half the noodles in bottom of greased 13×9-inch baking pan. Spread half the cottage cheese mixture over noodles, then half the meat mixture and half the Cheddar cheese and mozzarella cheese. Repeat layers. Sprinkle with remaining ¼ cup Parmesan cheese.

6. Bake lasagna 40 to 45 minutes or until bubbly. Let stand 10 minutes before cutting.

Makes 8 to 10 servings

Note: Lasagna may be assembled, covered and refrigerated up to 2 days in advance. Bake, uncovered, in preheated 375°F oven 60 minutes or until bubbly.

Lasagna Supreme

34

Hungarian Goulash Casserole

1 pound ground pork
¼ teaspoon salt
¼ teaspoon black pepper
¼ teaspoon ground nutmeg
1 tablespoon vegetable oil
1 cup reduced-fat sour cream, divided
1 tablespoon cornstarch
1 can (10¾ ounces) cream of celery soup
1 cup milk
1 teaspoon sweet Hungarian paprika
1 package (12 ounces) egg noodles, cooked and drained
2 teaspoons minced fresh dill (optional)

1. Preheat oven to 325°F. Spray 13×9-inch casserole dish with nonstick cooking spray.

2. Combine pork, salt, pepper and nutmeg in bowl. Shape into 1-inch meatballs. Heat oil in large skillet over medium-high heat. Add meatballs. Cook 10 minutes or until browned on all sides and no longer pink in center. Remove meatballs from skillet; discard drippings.

3. Stir together ¼ cup sour cream and cornstarch in small bowl. Spoon into same skillet. Add remaining sour cream, soup, milk and paprika. Stir until smooth.

4. Spoon cooked noodles into prepared dish. Arrange meatballs over noodles and cover with sauce. Bake 20 minutes or until hot. Sprinkle with dill if desired.   *Make 4 to 6 servings*

Hungarian Goulash Casserole

Veg•All® Beef & Cheddar Bake

2 cans (15 ounces each) VEG•ALL® Original Mixed Vegetables, drained
3 cups shredded Cheddar cheese
2 cups cooked elbow macaroni
1 pound extra-lean ground beef, cooked and drained
½ cup chopped onion
¼ teaspoon pepper

1. Preheat oven to 350°F.

2. In large mixing bowl, combine Veg•All, cheese, macaroni, ground beef, onion and pepper; mix well. Pour mixture into large casserole. Bake for 30 to 35 minutes. Serve hot.

Makes 4 to 6 servings

Old-Fashioned Beef Pot Pie

1 pound ground beef
1 can (11 ounces) condensed beef with vegetables and barley soup
½ cup water
1 package (10 ounces) frozen peas and carrots, thawed and drained
½ teaspoon seasoned salt
⅛ teaspoon garlic powder
⅛ teaspoon ground black pepper
1 cup (4 ounces) shredded Cheddar cheese, divided
1⅓ cups *French's*® French Fried Onions, divided
1 package (7½ ounces) refrigerated biscuits

Preheat oven to 350°F. In large skillet, brown ground beef in large chunks; drain. Stir in soup, water, vegetables and seasonings; bring to a boil. Reduce heat and simmer, uncovered, 5 minutes. Remove from heat; stir in ½ cup cheese and ⅔ *cup* French Fried Onions.

Pour mixture into 12×8-inch baking dish. Cut each biscuit in half; place, cut side down, around edge of casserole. Bake, uncovered, 15 to 20 minutes or until biscuits are done. Top with remaining cheese and ⅔ *cup* onions; bake, uncovered, 5 minutes or until onions are golden brown.

Makes 4 to 6 servings

Veg•All® Beef & Cheddar Bake

38

Easy Oven Beef Stew

        2 pounds boneless beef stew meat, cut into 1½-inch cubes
        1 can (16 ounces) tomatoes, undrained, cut up
        1 can (10½ ounces) condensed beef broth
        1 cup HOLLAND HOUSE® Red Cooking Wine
        1 tablespoon dried Italian seasonings*
        6 potatoes, peeled, quartered
        6 carrots cut into 2-inch pieces
        3 ribs celery cut into 1-inch pieces
        2 medium onions, peeled, quartered
        ⅓ cup instant tapioca
        ¼ teaspoon black pepper
          Chopped fresh parsley

*You may substitute 1½ teaspoons each of dried basil and oregano for Italian seasonings.

Heat oven to 325°F. Combine all ingredients except parsley in ovenproof Dutch oven; cover. Bake 2½ to 3 hours or until meat and vegetables are tender. Garnish with parsley.

Makes 8 servings

40

Spicy Lasagna Rollers

      1½ pounds Italian sausage, casings removed
        1 jar (28 ounces) spaghetti sauce, divided
        1 can (8 ounces) tomato sauce
        ½ cup chopped roasted red pepper
        ¾ teaspoon dried Italian seasoning
        ½ teaspoon red pepper flakes
        1 container (15 ounces) ricotta cheese
        1 package (10 ounces) frozen chopped spinach, thawed and squeezed dry
        2 cups (8 ounces) shredded Italian-blend cheese, divided
        1 cup (4 ounces) shredded Cheddar cheese, divided
        1 egg, lightly beaten
       12 lasagna noodles, cooked and drained

Preheat oven to 350°F. Spray 13×9-inch baking pan with nonstick cooking spray; set aside.

Cook sausage in large skillet over medium heat until browned, stirring to break up meat; drain. Stir in ½ cup spaghetti sauce, tomato sauce, roasted pepper, Italian seasoning and pepper flakes.

Mix ricotta, spinach, 1½ cups Italian-blend cheese, ½ cup Cheddar cheese and egg in medium bowl. Spread ¼ cup ricotta mixture over each noodle. Top with ⅓ cup sausage mixture. Tightly roll up each noodle from short end, jelly-roll style. Place rolls, seam sides down, in prepared pan. Pour remaining spaghetti sauce over rolls. Sprinkle with remaining ½ cup Italian-blend cheese and ½ cup Cheddar cheese. Cover pan with foil.

Bake 30 minutes. Remove foil and bake 15 minutes or until sauce is bubbly.

Makes 6 servings

Zucchini Pasta Bake

1½ cups uncooked pasta tubes
½ pound ground beef
½ cup chopped onion
1 clove garlic, minced
Salt and pepper
1 can (14½ ounces) DEL MONTE® Zucchini with Italian-Style Tomato Sauce
1 teaspoon dried basil, crushed
1 cup (4 ounces) shredded Monterey Jack cheese

1. Cook pasta according to package directions; drain.

2. Cook beef with onion and garlic in large skillet; drain. Season with salt and pepper.

3. Stir in zucchini with tomato sauce and basil. Place pasta in 8-inch square baking dish. Top with meat mixture.

4. Bake at 350°F for 15 minutes. Top with cheese. Bake 3 minutes or until cheese is melted.

Makes 4 servings

Prep and Cook Time: 33 minutes

41

Mexi-Tortilla Casserole

1 tablespoon vegetable oil
1 small onion, chopped
1 pound ground pork*
1 can (14½ ounces) diced tomatoes, undrained
1 teaspoon dried oregano, crushed
¼ teaspoon salt
¼ teaspoon ground cumin
¼ teaspoon pepper
1½ cups (6 ounces) shredded Cheddar Jack with jalapeño peppers or taco-style cheese
2 cups tortilla chips
½ cup reduced-fat sour cream
1 can (4 ounces) diced green chilies, drained
2 tablespoons minced cilantro

*For a vegetarian casserole, substitute 1 pound tofu crumbles for the pork.

42

1. Preheat oven to 350°F.

2. Heat oil in large skillet. Add onion and cook 5 minutes or until tender. Add pork and cook until brown, breaking up with spoon. Pour off fat. Stir in tomatoes with juice, oregano, salt, cumin and pepper. Spoon into 11×7-inch casserole. Sprinkle cheese over casserole; arrange tortilla chips over cheese. Bake 10 to 15 minutes or until cheese melts.

3. Combine sour cream and chilies; mix until well blended. Drop by tablespoonfuls over baked casserole. Sprinkle with cilantro.   *Makes 6 servings*

Cilantro is a green leafy herb that looks a lot like Italian parsley. Its distinctive flavor complements spicy foods, especially Mexican, Caribbean, Thai and Vietnamese dishes.

Mexi-Tortilla Casserole

Sweet and Savory Sausage Casserole

2 sweet potatoes, peeled and cut into 1-inch cubes
2 apples, peeled, cored and cut into 1-inch cubes
1 medium onion, cut into thin strips
2 tablespoons vegetable oil
2 teaspoons dried Italian seasoning
1 teaspoon garlic powder
½ teaspoon salt
½ teaspoon black pepper
1 pound cooked Italian sausage, cut into ½-inch pieces

Preheat oven to 400°F. Spray 13×9-inch baking pan with nonstick cooking spray.

Combine potatoes, apples, onion, oil, Italian seasoning, garlic powder, salt and pepper in large bowl. Toss to coat evenly. Place potato mixture into prepared pan. Bake, covered, 30 minutes. Add sausage to potato mixture; bake 5 to 10 minutes or until sausage is heated through and potatoes are tender.

Makes 4 to 6 servings

44

Creamy Beef and Vegetable Casserole

1 pound lean ground beef
1 small onion, chopped
1 bag (16 ounces) BIRDS EYE® frozen Farm Fresh Mixtures Broccoli, Corn & Red Peppers
1 can (10¾ ounces) cream of mushroom soup

- In medium skillet, brown beef and onion; drain excess fat.

- Meanwhile, in large saucepan, cook vegetables according to package directions; drain.

- Stir in beef mixture and soup. Cook over medium heat until heated through.

Makes 4 servings

Serving Suggestion: Serve over rice and sprinkle with ½ cup shredded Cheddar cheese.

Prep Time: 5 minutes
Cook Time: 10 to 15 minutes

Sweet and Savory Sausage Casserole

Quick Tamale Casserole

1½ pounds ground beef
¾ cup sliced green onions
1 can (4 ounces) chopped green chilies, drained and divided
1 can (16 ounces) whole kernel corn, drained
1 can (10¾ ounces) condensed tomato soup
¾ cup salsa
1 can (2¼ ounces) chopped pitted ripe olives (optional)
1 tablespoon Worcestershire sauce
1 teaspoon chili powder
¼ teaspoon garlic powder
4 slices (¾ ounce each) American cheese, halved
4 corn muffins, cut into ½-inch cubes
  Mexican Sour Cream Topping (recipe follows, optional)

Preheat oven to 350°F. Brown ground beef with green onions in medium skillet over medium-high heat. Reserve 2 tablespoons chilies for Mexican Sour Cream Topping. Stir remaining chilies, corn, tomato soup, salsa, olives, Worcestershire sauce, chili powder and garlic powder into skillet until well blended. Place in 2-quart casserole. Top with cheese, then evenly spread muffin cubes over cheese. Bake 5 to 10 minutes or until cheese is melted. Meanwhile, prepare Mexican Sour Cream Topping. Serve casserole with topping, if desired.   *Makes 6 servings*

Mexican Sour Cream Topping

1 cup sour cream
2 tablespoons chopped green chilies, reserved from above
2 teaspoons chopped jalapeño peppers* (optional)
2 teaspoons lime juice

*Jalapeño peppers can sting and irritate the skin; wear rubber gloves when handling peppers and do not touch eyes. Wash hands after handling peppers.

Combine all ingredients in small bowl; mix until well blended.   *Makes about 1 cup*

Quick Tamale Casserole

Creamy SPAM™ Broccoli Casserole

Nonstick cooking spray
1 (7-ounce) package elbow macaroni
2 cups frozen cut broccoli, thawed and drained
1 (12-ounce) can SPAM® Lite, cubed
½ cup chopped red bell pepper
2 cups skim milk
2 tablespoons cornstarch
¼ teaspoon black pepper
1 cup (4 ounces) shredded fat-free Cheddar cheese
¾ cup soft bread crumbs
2 teaspoons margarine, melted

Heat oven to 350°F. Spray 2-quart casserole with nonstick cooking spray. Cook macaroni according to package directions; drain. In prepared casserole, combine macaroni, broccoli, SPAM® and bell pepper. In small saucepan, stir together milk, cornstarch and black pepper until cornstarch is dissolved. Bring to a boil, stirring constantly, until thickened. Reduce heat to low. Add cheese; stir until melted. Stir sauce into SPAM™ mixture. Combine bread crumbs and margarine; sprinkle on top of casserole. Bake 40 minutes or until thoroughly heated.

Makes 8 servings

48

To make soft bread crumbs, choose firm-textured bread and remove the crusts from five slices. Tear the bread slices into small pieces and place them in a food processor. Process using an on/off pulsing action until the crumbs are the desired size. If the bread is very soft, lightly toast it before tearing it into pieces.

Creamy SPAM™ Broccoli Casserole

Tuna Pot Pie

1 tablespoon margarine or butter
1 small onion, chopped
1 can (10¾ ounces) condensed cream of potato soup, undiluted
¼ cup milk
½ teaspoon dried thyme leaves
¼ teaspoon salt
⅛ teaspoon black pepper
2 cans (6 ounces each) albacore tuna in water, drained
1 package (16 ounces) frozen vegetable medley, such as broccoli, green beans, carrots and
   red peppers, thawed
2 tablespoons chopped fresh parsley
1 can (8 ounces) refrigerated crescent roll dough

1. Preheat oven to 350°F. Spray 11×7-inch baking dish with nonstick cooking spray.

2. Melt margarine in large skillet over medium heat. Add onion; cook and stir 2 minutes or until onion is tender. Add soup, milk, thyme, salt and pepper; cook and stir 3 to 4 minutes or until thick and bubbly. Stir in tuna, vegetables and parsley. Pour mixture into prepared dish.

3. Unroll crescent roll dough and divide into triangles. Place triangles over tuna filling without overlapping dough.

4. Bake, uncovered, 20 minutes or until triangles are golden brown. Let stand 5 minutes before serving.   *Makes 6 servings*

Note: Experiment with different vegetable combinations and create an exciting recipe every time. Just substitute a new medley for the one listed and enjoy the results.

Tuna Pot Pie

Rigatoni Con Ricotta

1 package (16 ounces) BARILLA® Rigatoni
2 eggs
1 container (15 ounces) ricotta cheese
¾ cup (3 ounces) grated Parmesan cheese
1 tablespoon dried parsley
2 jars (26 ounces each) BARILLA® Lasagna & Casserole Sauce or Marinara Pasta Sauce, divided
3 cups (12 ounces) shredded mozzarella cheese, divided

1. Preheat oven to 375°F. Spray 13×9×2-inch baking pan with nonstick cooking spray. Cook rigatoni according to package directions; drain.

2. Beat eggs in small bowl. Stir in ricotta, Parmesan and parsley.

3. To assemble casserole, spread 2 cups lasagna sauce to cover bottom of pan. Place half of cooked rigatoni over sauce; top with half of ricotta mixture, dropped by spoonfuls. Layer with 1 cup mozzarella, 2 cups lasagna sauce, remaining rigatoni and ricotta mixture. Top with 1 cup mozzarella, remaining lasagna sauce and remaining 1 cup mozzarella.

4. Cover with foil and bake 60 to 70 minutes or until bubbly. Uncover and continue cooking about 5 minutes or until cheese is melted. Let stand 15 minutes before serving.

Makes 12 servings

52

Traditional Italian ricotta cheese is not really a cheese at all, because it is not made from milk, but instead from whey, a by-product of the cheese making process. American manufacturers often make ricotta cheese from a combination of whey and milk.

Rigatoni Con Ricotta

Classic Stuffed Shells

1 jar (26 to 28 ounces) RAGÚ® Old World Style® Pasta Sauce, divided
2 pounds part-skim ricotta cheese
2 cups part-skim shredded mozzarella cheese (about 8 ounces)
¼ cup grated Parmesan cheese
3 eggs
1 tablespoon finely chopped fresh parsley
⅛ teaspoon ground black pepper
1 box (12 ounces) jumbo shells pasta, cooked and drained

Preheat oven to 350°F. In 13×9-inch baking pan, evenly spread 1 cup Ragú® Old World Style Pasta Sauce; set aside.

In large bowl, combine cheeses, eggs, parsley and black pepper. Fill shells with cheese mixture, then arrange in baking pan. Evenly top with remaining sauce. Bake 45 minutes or until sauce is bubbling.   *Makes 8 servings*

54

Cheesy Broccoli 'n Mushroom Bake

2 packages (10 ounces each) frozen broccoli spears, thawed
1 can (10¾ ounces) condensed cream of mushroom soup
½ cup MIRACLE WHIP® Salad Dressing
½ cup milk
1 cup KRAFT® Shredded Cheddar Cheese
½ cup coarsely crushed croutons

• ARRANGE broccoli in 12×8-inch baking dish.

• WHISK together soup, salad dressing and milk. Pour over broccoli. Sprinkle with cheese and croutons.

• BAKE at 350°F for 30 to 35 minutes or until thoroughly heated.   *Makes 6 to 8 servings*

Prep Time: 10 minutes
Bake Time: 35 minutes

Classic Stuffed Shells

Penne Tuna Casserole

1 package (16 ounces) uncooked BARILLA® Mini Penne
1 jar (26 ounces) BARILLA® Lasagna & Casserole Sauce
2 cans (6 ounces each) tuna, drained and separated into chunks
1½ cups shredded mozzarella cheese
3 tablespoons grated Parmesan cheese
   Chopped parsley, for garnish

Preheat oven to 350°F.

Prepare penne according to package directions; drain.

Combine penne with BARILLA® sauce and tuna in 12×8-inch casserole and mix well. Sprinkle with cheeses and bake 40 minutes or until heated through and chesses are melted. Place casserole under broiler briefly to brown cheese, if desired. Garnish with chopped parsley, if desired. Serve immediately.
Makes 4 to 6 servings

Wisconsin Cheese Pasta Casserole

1 pound spaghetti or fettuccine, broken into 3-inch pieces
1 quart prepared spaghetti sauce
½ cup plus ⅓ cup grated Wisconsin Romano cheese, divided
1¾ cups (7 ounces) sliced or shredded Wisconsin Colby cheese
1½ cups (6 ounces) shredded Wisconsin Mozzarella cheese

Prepare pasta according to package instructions: drain. Toss warm pasta with prepared spaghetti sauce to coat. Add ½ cup Romano cheese to mixture and mix well. Spread half of sauced pasta into bottom of a 13×9×2-inch baking dish. Cover with 1 cup of Colby cheese. Spread remaining pasta over cheese. Top with remaining ¾ cup Colby cheese. Sprinkle with remaining ⅓ cup Romano cheese and Mozzarella cheese. Bake at 350°F for 35 to 40 minutes or until top is lightly browned and casserole is bubbly. Remove from heat and let stand at least 10 minutes before serving.
Makes 6 to 8 servings

*Favorite recipe from **Wisconsin Milk Marketing Board***

Veggie Pie with Cucina Classica™ Parmesan Cheese

  2 tablespoons olive oil
  2 large carrots, thinly sliced
  4 shallots, sliced or 2 bunches (about 15) scallions,* cut into ½-inch pieces
15 fresh green beans,* cut in half
  6 eggs, beaten or equivalent egg substitute
½ cup low fat milk
  1 tablespoon all-purpose flour
½ teaspoon salt
⅛ teaspoon pepper
½ cup CUCINA CLASSICA™ Grated Parmesan cheese

*One-half cup peas can be substituted for green beans; medium yellow onion can be substituted for shallots.

Preheat oven to 350°F. Grease 9-inch square baking dish or 9-inch quiche pan. Set aside.

In large skillet, heat olive oil over medium heat. Add carrots, shallots and beans. Cook 5 minutes or until shallots are glossy and carrots and beans are tender-crisp, stirring occasionally. Drain off any excess oil.

In large mixing bowl, mix eggs, milk, flour, salt, pepper and Cucina Classica™ grated Parmesan cheese. Stir in vegetables. Pour into prepared baking dish. Bake 15 to 20 minutes or until set.

Makes 4 servings

57

Shallots belong to the same family as onions. Each shallot head is made up of two or three cloves, and each clove is covered in a papery skin that ranges in color from reddish tan to gold. The flesh is off-white with a hint of purple.

Tuna Noodle Casserole

7 ounces uncooked elbow macaroni
2 tablespoons margarine or butter
¾ cup chopped onion
½ cup thinly sliced celery
½ cup finely chopped red bell pepper
2 tablespoons all-purpose flour
1 teaspoon salt
⅛ teaspoon white pepper
1½ cups milk
1 can (6 ounces) albacore tuna in water, drained
½ cup grated Parmesan cheese, divided
   Fresh dill sprigs (optional)

1. Preheat oven to 375°F. Spray 8-inch square baking dish with nonstick cooking spray.

2. Cook pasta according to package directions until al dente. Drain and set aside.

3. Meanwhile, melt margarine in large deep skillet over medium heat. Add onion; cook and stir 3 minutes. Add celery and bell pepper; cook and stir 3 minutes. Sprinkle flour, salt and white pepper over vegetables; cook and stir 1 minute. Gradually stir in milk; cook and stir until thickened. Remove from heat.

4. Add pasta, tuna and ¼ cup cheese to skillet; stir until pasta is well coated. Pour tuna mixture into prepared dish; sprinkle evenly with remaining ¼ cup cheese.

5. Bake, uncovered, 20 to 25 minutes or until hot and bubbly. Garnish with dill, if desired.

Makes 4 servings

Tuna Noodle Casserole

Cheesy Broccoli Bake

1 (10-ounce) package frozen chopped broccoli
1 (10¾-ounce) can condensed Cheddar cheese soup
½ cup sour cream
2 cups (12 ounces) chopped CURE 81® ham
2 cups cooked rice
½ cup soft, torn bread crumbs
1 tablespoon butter or margarine, melted

Heat oven to 350°F. Cook broccoli according to package directions; drain. Combine soup and sour cream. Stir in broccoli, ham and rice. Spoon into 1½-quart casserole. Combine bread crumbs and butter; sprinkle over casserole. Bake 30 to 35 minutes or until thoroughly heated.

Makes 4 to 6 servings

Pasta with Four Cheeses

¾ cup uncooked ziti or rigatoni
3 tablespoons butter, divided
½ cup grated CUCINA CLASSICA ITALIANA® Parmesan cheese, divided
¼ teaspoon ground nutmeg, divided
¼ cup GALBANI® Mascarpone
¾ cup (about 3½ ounces) shredded mozzarella cheese
¾ cup (about 3½ ounces) shredded BEL PAESE® semi-soft cheese

Preheat oven to 350°F. Lightly grease 1-quart casserole. Set aside.

In large saucepan of boiling water, cook pasta until tender but still firm. Drain in colander. Place in large mixing bowl. Stir in 1½ tablespoons butter, ¼ cup Parmesan cheese and ⅛ teaspoon nutmeg.

Spread one fourth of pasta mixture into prepared casserole. Spoon Mascarpone onto pasta. Layer with one fourth of pasta. Top with mozzarella. Add third layer of pasta. Sprinkle with Bel Paese® cheese. Top with remaining pasta. Dot with 1½ tablespoons butter. Sprinkle with remaining ¼ cup Parmesan cheese and ⅛ teaspoon nutmeg. Bake until golden brown, about 20 minutes.

Makes 4 servings

Cheesy Broccoli Bake

Easy Crab-Asparagus Pie

   4 ounces crabmeat, shredded
 12 ounces fresh asparagus, cooked
   ½ cup chopped onion, cooked
   1 cup (4 ounces) shredded Monterey Jack cheese
   ¼ cup grated Parmesan cheese
      Black pepper
   ¾ cup all-purpose flour
   ¾ teaspoon baking powder
   ½ teaspoon salt
   2 tablespoons butter or margarine, chilled
1½ cups milk
   4 eggs, lightly beaten

1. Preheat oven to 350°F. Lightly grease 10-inch quiche dish or pie plate.

2. Layer crabmeat, asparagus and onion in prepared pie plate; top with cheeses. Season with pepper.

3. Combine flour, baking powder and salt in large bowl. With pastry blender or 2 knives, cut in butter until mixture forms coarse crumbs. Stir in milk and eggs; pour over vegetables and cheeses.

4. Bake 30 minutes or until filling is puffed and knife inserted near center comes out clean. Serve hot. *Makes 6 servings*

Spinach-Cheese Pasta Casserole

   8 ounces uncooked pasta shells
   2 eggs
   1 cup ricotta cheese
   1 package (10 ounces) frozen chopped spinach, thawed and squeezed dry
   1 jar (26 ounces) marinara sauce
   1 teaspoon salt
   1 cup (4 ounces) shredded mozzarella cheese
   ¼ cup grated Parmesan cheese

Preheat oven to 350°F. Spray 1½-quart round casserole with nonstick cooking spray.

Cook pasta according to package directions until al dente. Drain.

Meanwhile, whisk eggs in large bowl until blended. Add ricotta and spinach to eggs; stir until combined. Stir in pasta, marinara sauce and salt until pasta is well coated. Pour into prepared dish. Sprinkle mozzarella and Parmesan evenly over casserole.

Bake, covered, 30 minutes. Uncover and bake 15 minutes or until hot and bubbly.

Makes 6 to 8 servings

Meatless Ravioli Bake

    4 cups finely chopped eggplant
½ cup chopped onion
¼ cup chopped carrots
¼ cup chopped celery
    3 tablespoons olive oil
    2 cans (8 ounces each) HUNT'S® No Salt Added Tomato Sauce
    1 can (14.5 ounces) HUNT'S® Crushed Tomatoes
½ teaspoon sugar
⅛ teaspoon pepper
    1 package (18 ounces) frozen large ravioli, prepared according to package directions

1. Preheat oven to 375°F.

2. In saucepan, sauté eggplant, onion, carrots and celery in hot oil; cook until tender.

3. Stir in Hunt's Tomato Sauce, Hunt's Tomatoes, sugar and pepper. Simmer, uncovered, 10 minutes; stirring occasionally.

4. Spoon *1½ cups* of tomato mixture into 13×9×2-inch baking dish; top with half the ravioli and *half* of the *remaining* sauce. Repeat layers.

5. Bake, uncovered, 30 minutes or until bubbly.

Makes 6 (7-ounce) servings

63

Manicotti Marinara

1 package (8 ounces) BARILLA® Manicotti *or* ½ package (8 ounces) BARILLA® Jumbo Shells
2 jars (26 ounces each) BARILLA® Marinara Pasta Sauce, divided
2 eggs
1 container (15 ounces) ricotta cheese
4 cups (16 ounces) shredded mozzarella cheese, divided
1 cup (4 ounces) grated Parmesan cheese, divided
¼ cup chopped fresh parsley *or* 1 tablespoon dried parsley

1. Cook manicotti shells according to package directions; drain. Preheat oven to 350°F. Spray bottom of 15×10×2-inch glass baking dish with nonstick cooking spray. Spread 1 jar marinara sauce over bottom of baking dish.

2. Beat eggs in large bowl. Stir in ricotta, 3 cups mozzarella, ¾ cup Parmesan and parsley. Fill each cooked shell with ricotta mixture. Arrange filled shells in baking dish over sauce. Top with second jar of marinara sauce, remaining 1 cup mozzarella and ¼ cup Parmesan.

3. Cover with foil and bake about 45 minutes or until bubbly. Uncover and continue baking about 5 minutes or until cheese is melted. Let stand 5 minutes before serving.

Makes 6 servings

Note: One package (10 ounces) frozen chopped spinach, thawed and well drained, may be added to the ricotta mixture.

To fill a manicotti shell, hold it in one hand and fill it using a small spoon or long-handled iced tea spoon. Fill from one end and push the filling to the center of the shell, then turn and finish filling from the other end.

64

Manicotti Marinara

Creamy Chicken and Mushrooms

   1 teaspoon salt
½ teaspoon black pepper
¼ teaspoon paprika
   3 boneless skinless chicken breasts, cut up
1¾ teaspoons chicken bouillon granules
1½ cups sliced fresh mushrooms, drained
½ cup sliced green onions
   1 cup white wine
½ cup water
   1 can (5 ounces) evaporated milk
   5 teaspoons cornstarch
   Hot cooked rice

SLOW COOKER DIRECTIONS

1. Combine salt, pepper and paprika in small bowl; sprinkle over chicken. Rub spices into chicken.

2. Layer chicken, bouillon, mushrooms and green onions in slow cooker. Pour wine and water over top. Cover; cook on HIGH 3 hours or on LOW 5 to 6 hours. Remove chicken and vegetables to platter; cover to keep warm.

3. Combine evaporated milk and cornstarch in small saucepan until smooth. Gradually stir in 2 cups liquid from slow cooker. Bring to a boil. Boil 1 minute or until thickened, stirring constantly. To serve, spoon sauce over chicken and rice.

Makes 3 to 4 servings

Come home to a delicious, satisfying meal when you prepare dinner in a slow cooker. Everyone will agree, it's a great way to begin an evening.

Creamy Chicken and Mushrooms

Chicken and Stuffing

½ cup all-purpose flour
¾ teaspoon seasoned salt
  Black pepper, to taste
4 to 6 boneless skinless chicken breasts
¼ cup butter
2 cans (10¾ ounces each) condensed cream of mushroom soup, undiluted
½ cup water
1 package (12 ounces) seasoned stuffing mix

SLOW COOKER DIRECTIONS

Combine flour, seasoned salt and pepper in large resealable food storage bag. Dredge chicken in flour mixture. Melt butter in large skillet over medium-low heat. Brown both sides of chicken in butter. Place chicken in slow cooker. Combine soup and water in medium bowl; pour over chicken. Prepare stuffing mix according to package directions, decreasing liquid by half; arrange over chicken. Cover; cook on HIGH 3 to 4 hours. *Makes 4 to 6 servings*

68

He-Man Stew

1 package (about 3½ pounds) PERDUE® Fresh Skinless Pick of the Chicken
  Salt and black pepper, to taste
2 tablespoons olive oil
1 can (28 ounces) whole plum tomatoes, drained and chopped
1 can (12 ounces) lite beer
1 onion, sliced into rings
¼ cup spicy brown mustard
4 cups cooked elbow macaroni

SLOW COOKER DIRECTIONS

Season chicken with salt and pepper. In large skillet over medium-high heat, heat oil. Cook chicken 5 to 6 minutes per side (larger pieces), 3 to 4 minutes per side (smaller pieces), or until brown, turning often. In large slow cooker, combine tomatoes, beer, onion and mustard. Add chicken. Cook on HIGH 1½ to 2 hours, or until chicken is fork-tender. Serve over macaroni.

Makes 3 to 4 servings

Chicken and Stuffing

Turkey Tacos

1 pound ground turkey
1 medium onion, chopped
1 can (6 ounces) tomato paste
½ cup chunky salsa
1 tablespoon chopped fresh cilantro
½ teaspoon salt
8 taco shells
1 tablespoon butter
1 tablespoon all-purpose flour
¼ teaspoon salt
⅓ cup milk
½ cup sour cream
Dash ground red pepper

SLOW COOKER DIRECTIONS

Cook turkey and onion in large skillet over medium heat until turkey is brown, stirring to separate turkey. Combine turkey mixture, tomato paste, salsa, cilantro and salt in slow cooker. Cover and cook on LOW 4 to 5 hours.

Just before serving, melt butter in small saucepan over low heat. Stir in flour and salt; cook 1 minute. Carefully stir in milk. Cook over low heat until thickened. Remove from heat. Combine sour cream and ground red pepper in small bowl. Stir into hot milk mixture. Return to heat; cook over low heat 1 minute, stirring constantly.

Spoon ¼ cup turkey mixture into each taco shell. Spoon sauce over taco filling.

Makes 8 tacos

Helpful Hint

Keep the lid on the slow cooker! It takes between 20 and 30 minutes for a slow cooker to regain the heat lost when the lid is removed.

70

Harvest Drums

1 package (about 1¼ pounds) PERDUE® Fresh Skinless Chicken Drumsticks
½ teaspoon dried Italian herb seasoning
   Salt and ground pepper
3 bacon slices, diced
2 cans (14½ ounces each) pasta-ready tomatoes with cheeses
1 small onion, chopped
¼ cup red wine
1 clove garlic, minced
1 small zucchini, scrubbed and julienned
1 package (12 ounces) angel hair pasta, cooked and drained

SLOW COOKER DIRECTIONS
Sprinkle chicken with Italian seasoning and salt and pepper to taste. In large, nonstick skillet over medium-low heat, cook bacon about 5 minutes, until crisp. Remove from skillet; drain and crumble. Increase heat to medium-high. Add chicken to bacon drippings (or replace drippings with 1½ tablespoons olive oil); cook 4 to 5 minutes on all sides or until brown, turning often.

71

In large slow cooker, combine tomatoes, bacon, onion, wine and garlic. Add chicken; cook on HIGH 1½ to 1¾ hours, or until fork-tender. Add zucchini during last 5 minutes of cooking. Serve chicken and vegetables over angel hair pasta.   *Makes 3 to 4 servings*

Chicken skin tends to shrivel and curl in the moist heat of a slow cooker. That's why most recipes call for skinless chicken. If you use skin-on pieces, brown them in a skillet in a little oil before adding them to the slow cooker. This will give the chicken more flavor and reduce curling.

Three-Bean Turkey Chili

1 pound ground turkey
1 small onion, chopped
1 can (28 ounces) diced tomatoes, undrained
1 can (about 14 ounces) chick-peas
1 can (about 14 ounces) kidney beans
1 can (about 14 ounces) black beans
1 can (8 ounces) tomato sauce
1 can (about 4 ounces) chopped mild green chilies
1 to 2 tablespoons chili powder

SLOW COOKER DIRECTIONS

1. Cook turkey and onion in medium skillet over medium-high heat, stirring to break up meat, until turkey is no longer pink. Drain; place turkey mixture in slow cooker.

2. Add all remaining ingredients and mix well. Cook on HIGH 6 to 8 hours.

Makes 6 to 8 servings

72

Simple Coq au Vin

4 chicken legs
 Salt and black pepper
2 tablespoons olive oil
½ pound mushrooms, sliced
 1 onion, sliced into rings
½ cup red wine
½ teaspoon *each* dried basil leaves, dried thyme leaves and dried oregano leaves

SLOW COOKER DIRECTIONS

Sprinkle chicken with salt and pepper. Heat oil in large skillet; brown chicken on both sides. Remove chicken and place in slow cooker. Sauté mushrooms and onion in same skillet. Add wine; stir and scrape brown bits from bottom of skillet. Add mixture to slow cooker. Sprinkle with basil, thyme and oregano. Cover and cook on LOW 8 to 10 hours or on HIGH 3 to 4 hours. Serve chicken and sauce over hot cooked rice. *Makes 4 servings*

Three-Bean Turkey Chili

Slow Cooker Chicken & Rice

3 cans (10¾ ounces each) condensed cream of chicken soup, undiluted
2 cups instant rice
1 cup water
1 pound boneless skinless chicken breasts or breast tenders
   Salt and black pepper, to taste
   Paprika, to taste
½ cup diced celery

SLOW COOKER DIRECTIONS
Combine soup, rice and water in slow cooker. Add chicken; sprinkle with salt, pepper and paprika. Add celery. Cover and cook on HIGH 3 to 4 hours or on LOW 6 to 8 hours.

Makes 4 servings

Chicken Parisienne

6 boneless skinless chicken breasts, cubed
   Salt, to taste
   Black pepper, to taste
½ teaspoon paprika
1 can (10¾ ounces) condensed cream of mushroom or cream of chicken soup, undiluted
2 cans (4 ounces each) sliced mushrooms, drained
½ cup dry white wine
1 cup sour cream
6 cups hot cooked egg noodles

SLOW COOKER DIRECTIONS
1. Place chicken cubes in slow cooker. Sprinkle with salt, pepper and paprika.

2. Pour soup, mushrooms and wine over chicken; mix well. Cover and cook on HIGH 2 to 3 hours. In last 30 minutes of cooking, add sour cream. Serve over noodles. Garnish as desired.

Makes 6 servings

Brunswick Stew

1 package (about 2 pounds) PERDUE® Fresh Chicken Thighs
2 cans (14½ ounces each) chicken broth
3 potatoes, peeled and diced into ½-inch pieces (3 cups)
1 can (14½ ounces) Cajun- or Mexican-style tomatoes
1 package (10 ounces) frozen succotash, partially thawed
   Salt and ground black pepper, to taste
   Hot pepper sauce, to taste

SLOW COOKER DIRECTIONS

In slow cooker, combine chicken, chicken broth and potatoes. Cover and cook on LOW heat 2½ to 3 hours until chicken is cooked through. Add tomatoes, succotash, salt and pepper. Turn heat to HIGH; cover and cook 1 hour. Season with salt, pepper and hot pepper sauce. Serve in soup bowls.   *Makes 4 to 6 servings*

Note: This recipe can also be cooked in a Dutch oven on top of the stove over medium-low heat for about 1 hour. For added flavor, stir in ½ cup diced PERDUE® Turkey Ham.

Brunswick stew is named for the county in Virginia in which it is said to have originated. Commonly made with chicken, it also includes tomatoes, lima beans and corn (succotash), and sometimes okra. Brunswick stew was originally made with squirrel meat rather than chicken.

Country Captain Chicken

4 chicken thighs
2 tablespoons all-purpose flour
2 tablespoons vegetable oil, divided
1 cup chopped green bell pepper
1 large onion, chopped
1 rib celery, chopped
1 clove garlic, minced
¼ cup chicken broth
2 cups canned crushed tomatoes or diced fresh tomatoes
½ cup golden raisins
1½ teaspoons curry powder
1 teaspoon salt
¼ teaspoon paprika
¼ teaspoon black pepper
2 cups hot cooked rice

SLOW COOKER DIRECTIONS

1. Coat chicken with flour; set aside. Heat 1 tablespoon oil in large skillet over medium-high heat until hot. Add bell pepper, onion, celery and garlic. Cook and stir 5 minutes or until vegetables are tender. Place vegetables in slow cooker.

2. Heat remaining 1 tablespoon oil in same skillet over medium-high heat. Add chicken and cook 5 minutes per side. Place chicken in slow cooker.

3. Pour broth into skillet. Heat over medium-high heat, stirring frequently and scraping up any browned bits from bottom of skillet. Pour liquid into slow cooker. Add tomatoes, raisins, curry powder, salt, paprika and black pepper. Cover and cook on LOW 3 hours. Serve chicken with sauce over rice. *Makes 4 servings*

77

Country Captain is a traditional southern dish. Legend says that a British sea captain enjoyed this dish while he was stationed in India in the early 1800's and later shared it with friends in the port city of Savannah, Georgia. Interest in this dish spread to other parts of the country during World War II when newspapers reported that it was served to President Franklin Roosevelt and his guest, General George Patton, in Warm Springs, Georgia.

Chinese Cashew Chicken

1 pound fresh bean sprouts *or* 1 can (16 ounces) bean sprouts, drained
2 cups sliced cooked chicken
1 can (10¾ ounces) condensed cream of mushroom soup, undiluted
1 cup sliced celery
½ cup chopped green onion
1 can (4 ounces) mushroom pieces, drained
3 tablespoons butter
1 tablespoon soy sauce
1 cup cashews

SLOW COOKER DIRECTIONS
Combine all ingredients except cashews in slow cooker. Cover and cook on LOW 4 to 6 hours or on HIGH 3 to 4 hours. Just before serving, stir in cashews.   *Makes 4 servings*

78

Continental Chicken

1 package (2¼ ounces) dried beef, cut up
4 boneless skinless chicken breasts
4 slices lean bacon
1 can (10¾ ounces) condensed cream of mushroom soup, undiluted
¼ cup all-purpose flour
¼ cup low-fat sour cream

SLOW COOKER DIRECTIONS
1. Spray inside of slow cooker with nonstick cooking spray. Place dried beef in bottom of slow cooker. Wrap each piece of chicken with one bacon strip. Place wrapped chicken on top of dried beef.

2. Combine soup, flour and sour cream in medium bowl; mix until smooth. Pour over chicken. Cover and cook on LOW 7 to 9 hours or on HIGH 3 to 4 hours.   *Makes 4 servings*

Chinese Cashew Chicken

Coconut Chicken Curry

1 tablespoon vegetable oil
4 boneless skinless chicken breasts
3 medium potatoes, peeled and chopped
1 medium onion, cut into slices
1 can (14 ounces) coconut milk
1 cup chicken broth
1½ teaspoons curry powder
1 teaspoon hot pepper sauce (optional)
½ teaspoon salt
½ teaspoon black pepper
1 package (10 ounces) frozen peas
   Hot cooked rice (optional)

SLOW COOKER DIRECTIONS

1. Heat oil in medium skillet. Brown chicken breasts on both sides. Place potatoes and onion in slow cooker. Place chicken breasts on top. Combine coconut milk, broth, curry powder, hot pepper sauce, if desired, salt and pepper in medium bowl. Pour over chicken. Cover; cook on LOW 6 to 8 hours.

2. About 30 minutes before serving, add peas to slow cooker. Serve over hot cooked rice, if desired.

Makes 4 servings

Helpful Hint

Coconut milk is used in many tropical and Asian dishes. It adds flavor to curries, puddings and sauces. Coconut milk is available in cans in Asian markets and some large supermarkets. It should not be confused with the juice that is drained from a fresh coconut before the meat is removed.

Coconut Chicken Curry

BBQ Pork Sandwiches

4 pounds boneless pork loin roast, fat trimmed
1 can (14½ ounces) beef broth
⅓ cup *French's*® Worcestershire Sauce
⅓ cup *Frank's*® *RedHot*® Cayenne Pepper Sauce

SAUCE
½ cup ketchup
½ cup molasses
¼ cup *French's*® Classic Yellow® Mustard
¼ cup *French's*® Worcestershire Sauce
2 tablespoons *Frank's*® *RedHot*® Cayenne Pepper Sauce

SLOW COOKER DIRECTIONS

1. Place roast on bottom of slow cooker. Combine broth, *⅓ cup each* Worcestershire and *Frank's RedHot* Sauce. Pour over roast. Cover and cook on high-heat setting 5 hours* or until roast is tender.

2. Meanwhile, combine ingredients for sauce in large bowl; set aside.

3. Transfer roast to large cutting board. Discard liquid. Coarsely chop roast. Stir into reserved sauce. Spoon pork mixture on large rolls. Serve with deli potato salad, if desired.

Makes 8 to 10 servings

*Or cook 10 hours on low-heat setting.

Tip: Make additional sauce and serve on the side. Great also with barbecued ribs and chops!

Prep Time: 10 minutes
Cook Time: 5 hours

82

BBQ Pork Sandwich

Easy Beef Stroganoff

3 cans (10¾ ounces each) condensed cream of chicken soup or condensed cream of
    mushroom soup, undiluted
1 cup sour cream
½ cup water
1 envelope (1 ounce) dried onion soup mix
2 pounds beef stew meat, cubed

SLOW COOKER DIRECTIONS
Combine soup, sour cream, water and onion soup mix in slow cooker. Add beef; stir until well
coated. Cover and cook on HIGH 3 hours or on LOW 6 hours.   *Makes 4 to 6 servings*

Note: Serve over rice or noodles with a tossed green salad and warm bread. You can reduce
the calories and fat by using reduced-fat soup and sour cream.

Campfire Sausage and Potato Soup

1 can (15½ ounces) dark kidney beans, rinsed and drained
1 can (14½ ounces) diced tomatoes, undrained
1 can (10½ ounces) condensed beef broth, undiluted
8 ounces kielbasa sausage, cut lengthwise into halves, then crosswise into ½-inch pieces
1 large baking potato, cut into ½-inch cubes
1 medium green bell pepper, diced
1 medium onion, diced
1 teaspoon dried oregano leaves
½ teaspoon sugar
1 to 2 teaspoons ground cumin

SLOW COOKER DIRECTIONS
Combine all ingredients, except cumin, in slow cooker. Cover and cook on LOW 8 hours or on
HIGH 4 hours. Stir in cumin; serve.   *Makes 6 to 7 servings*

Easy Beef Stroganoff

Slow Cooker Pepper Steak

2 tablespoons vegetable oil
3 pounds sirloin steak, cut into strips
1 heaping tablespoon (5 to 6 cloves) minced garlic
1 medium onion, chopped
½ cup reduced-sodium soy sauce
2 teaspoons sugar
1 teaspoon salt
½ teaspoon ground ginger
½ teaspoon black pepper
3 green bell peppers, cored, seeded and cut into strips
¼ cup cold water
1 tablespoon cornstarch
   Hot cooked white rice

SLOW COOKER DIRECTIONS

1. Heat oil in large skillet over medium-low heat. Brown steak on both sides; sprinkle garlic over top.

2. Transfer steak and pan juices to slow cooker. Add onion, soy sauce, sugar, salt, ginger and black pepper. Stir. Cover and cook on LOW 6 to 8 hours or until meat is tender (up to 10 hours).

3. In last hour of cooking, add bell pepper strips. Just before serving, mix together water and cornstarch; add to slow cooker. Cook on HIGH until sauce thickens. Serve over hot rice.

Makes 6 to 8 servings

Pork & Tomato Ragout

2 pounds boneless pork stew meat, cut into 1-inch pieces
¼ cup all-purpose flour
3 tablespoons olive oil
1¼ cups white wine
2 pounds red potatoes, cut into ½-inch pieces
1 can (14½ ounces) diced tomatoes, undrained
1 cup finely chopped onion
1 cup water
½ cup finely chopped celery
2 cloves garlic, minced
½ teaspoon black pepper
1 cinnamon stick
3 tablespoons chopped fresh parsley

SLOW COOKER DIRECTIONS

1. Toss pork with flour. Heat oil in large skillet. Add pork to skillet and cook until browned on all sides. Place pork in slow cooker.

2. Add wine to skillet; bring to a boil, scraping up browned bits from bottom of skillet. Pour into slow cooker.

3. Add all remaining ingredients except parsley. Cover; cook on LOW 6 to 8 hours or until pork and potatoes are tender. Remove and discard cinnamon stick. Sprinkle with parsley just before serving.   *Makes 6 servings*

Inexpensive cuts of meat work well in slow cooker recipes. Top-quality cuts, such as loin chops or filet mignon, tend to fall apart during long moist cooking.

Pork & Tomato Ragout

Farmhouse Ham and Vegetable Chowder

2 cans (10½ ounces each) cream of celery soup
2 cups diced cooked ham
1 package (10 ounces) frozen corn
1 large baking potato, cut in ½-inch pieces
1 medium red bell pepper, diced
½ teaspoon dried thyme leaves
2 cups small broccoli florets
½ cup milk

SLOW COOKER DIRECTIONS

1. Combine all ingredients, except broccoli and milk in slow cooker; stir to blend. Cover and cook on LOW 6 to 8 hours or on HIGH 3 to 4 hours.

2. If cooking on LOW, turn to HIGH and stir in broccoli and milk. Cover and cook 15 minutes or until broccoli is crisp-tender.
Makes 6 servings

90

1-2-3-4 Chili

2 pounds ground beef, browned and drained of fat
4 cans (8 ounces each) tomato sauce
3 cans (15 ounces each) chili-spiced kidney beans

SLOW COOKER DIRECTIONS

Combine all ingredients in slow cooker. Cook on LOW 6 to 8 hours. Garnish with cheese and green onion slices, if desired.
Makes 8 servings

Farmhouse Ham and Vegetable Chowder

Lamb in Dill Sauce

   2 large red-skinned potatoes, peeled and cut into 1-inch cubes
   ½ cup chopped onion
1½ teaspoons salt
   ½ teaspoon black pepper
   ½ teaspoon dried dill weed *or* 4 sprigs fresh dill
   1 bay leaf
   2 pounds lean lamb stew meat (1-inch cubes)
   1 cup plus 3 tablespoons water, divided
   2 tablespoons all-purpose flour
   1 teaspoon sugar
   2 tablespoons lemon juice
      Fresh dill (optional)

SLOW COOKER DIRECTIONS

Layer ingredients in slow cooker in the following order: potatoes, onion, salt, pepper, dill, bay leaf, lamb and 1 cup water. Cover and cook on LOW 6 to 8 hours.

Remove lamb and potatoes with slotted spoon; cover and keep warm. Remove and discard bay leaf. Turn heat to HIGH. Stir remaining 3 tablespoons water into flour in small bowl until smooth. Add half of cooking juices and sugar. Mix well and return to slow cooker. Cover and cook 15 minutes. Stir in lemon juice. Return lamb and potatoes to slow cooker. Cover and cook 10 minutes or until heated through. Garnish with fresh dill, if desired.

Makes 6 servings

When cooking vegetables in a slow cooker, they should be uniform in size and shape for even cooking. Always cut vegetables as recommended in the recipe.

Lamb in Dill Sauce

Red Beans and Rice with Ham

    1 package (1 pound) dried red beans
    1 pound beef sausage, sliced
    1 ham slice, cubed (about 8 ounces)
    1 small onion, diced
  2½ to 3 cups water
    Ground red pepper, to taste
    1 teaspoon adobo seasoning with pepper
    Hot cooked rice

SLOW COOKER DIRECTIONS

1. Soak beans in water overnight; rinse and drain.

2. Place beans in slow cooker. Add sausage, ham, onion and water (3 cups for HIGH; 2½ cups for LOW). Season with red pepper and adobo seasoning.

3. Cover and cook on HIGH 3 to 4 hours or on LOW 7 to 8 hours, stirring every 2 hours, if necessary. Serve over rice. *Makes 6 servings*

94

Spicy Beef and Pepper Fajitas

  1½ pounds beef flank steak, cut into 6 pieces
    1 cup chopped onion
    2 green bell peppers, cut into ½-inch-wide strips
    1 jalapeño pepper,* chopped
    2 tablespoons chopped fresh cilantro
    2 cloves garlic, minced
    1 teaspoon chili powder
    1 teaspoon ground cumin
    ½ teaspoon salt
    ¼ teaspoon ground red pepper
    1 can (8 ounces) chopped tomatoes, drained
   12 (8-inch) flour tortillas
    Toppings such as sour cream, shredded Cheddar cheese, salsa
    Sliced avocado (optional)

*Jalapeño peppers can sting and irritate the skin; wear rubber gloves when handling peppers and do not touch eyes. Wash hands after handling peppers.

SLOW COOKER DIRECTIONS

Combine beef, onion, bell peppers, jalapeño pepper, cilantro, garlic, chili powder, cumin, salt and ground red pepper in slow cooker. Add tomatoes. Cover and cook on LOW 8 to 10 hours.

Remove beef from slow cooker and pull into shreds with fork. Return beef to slow cooker. To serve, place beef mixture on tortillas. Top with suggested toppings; roll up tortillas. Serve with sliced avocado, if desired.   *Makes 12 servings*

Italian Combo Subs

1 tablespoon vegetable oil
1 pound round steak, cut into thin strips
1 pound bulk Italian sausage
1 medium onion, thinly sliced
1 can (4 ounces) sliced mushrooms (optional)
1 green bell pepper, cored, seeded and cut into strips
  Salt
  Black pepper
1 jar (25 ounces) spaghetti sauce
2 loaves Italian bread, cut into 1-inch-thick slices

SLOW COOKER DIRECTIONS

1. Heat oil in large skillet over medium-high heat. Brown round steak. Remove steak strips to slow cooker. Drain excess fat from skillet.

2. In same skillet, brown Italian sausage until no longer pink. Drain excess fat. Add sausage to slow cooker.

3. Place onion, mushrooms and bell pepper over meat. Add salt and black pepper to taste; cover with spaghetti sauce. Cover and cook on LOW 4 to 6 hours. Serve as a sandwich or over bread slices   *Makes 6 servings*

Serving Suggestion. Top with freshly grated Parmesan cheese.

Beef Stew with Molasses and Raisins

⅓ cup all-purpose flour
2 teaspoons salt, divided
1½ teaspoons black pepper, divided
2 pounds boneless beef chuck roast, cut into 1½-inch cubes
5 tablespoons canola oil, divided
2 medium onions, sliced
1 can (28 ounces) diced tomatoes, drained
1 cup beef broth
3 tablespoons molasses
2 tablespoons cider vinegar
4 cloves garlic, minced
2 teaspoons dried thyme leaves
1 teaspoon celery salt
1 bay leaf
8 ounces baby carrots, cut in half lengthwise
2 parsnips, diced
½ cup golden raisins
Salt and black pepper, to taste

SLOW COOKER DIRECTIONS

1. Combine flour, 1½ teaspoons salt and 1 teaspoon pepper in large bowl. Toss meat in flour mixture. Heat 2 tablespoons oil in large skillet over medium-high heat. Add half of beef and brown on all sides. Set aside browned beef and repeat with 2 tablespoons oil and remaining beef.

2. Add remaining 1 tablespoon oil to skillet. Add onions and cook, stirring to loosen any browned bits, about 5 minutes. Add tomatoes, broth, molasses, vinegar, garlic, thyme, celery salt, bay leaf and remaining ½ teaspoon salt and ½ teaspoon pepper. Bring to a boil. Add browned beef and boil 1 minute.

3. Transfer mixture to slow cooker. Cover and cook on LOW 5 hours or on HIGH 2½ hours. Add carrots, parsnips and raisins. Cook 1 to 2 hours more or until vegetables are tender. Remove and discard bay leaf. Season with salt and pepper. *Makes 6 to 8 servings*

Beef Stew with Molasses and Raisins

Smoked Sausage Gumbo

1 cup chicken broth
1 can (14½ ounces) diced tomatoes, undrained
¼ cup all-purpose flour
2 tablespoons olive oil
¾ pound Polish sausage, cut into ½-inch pieces
1 medium onion, diced
1 green bell pepper, diced
2 ribs celery, chopped
1 carrot, peeled and chopped
2 teaspoons dried oregano leaves
2 teaspoons dried thyme leaves
⅛ teaspoon ground red pepper
1 cup uncooked white rice

SLOW COOKER DIRECTIONS

Combine broth and tomatoes in slow cooker. Sprinkle flour evenly over bottom of small skillet. Cook over high heat with out stirring 3 to 4 minutes or until flour begins to brown. Reduce heat to medium; stir flour about 4 minutes. Stir in oil until smooth. Carefully whisk flour mixture into slow cooker.

Add sausage, onion, bell pepper, celery, carrot, oregano, thyme and ground red pepper to slow cooker. Stir well. Cover and cook on LOW 4½ to 5 hours or until juices are thickened.

About 30 minutes before gumbo is ready to serve, prepare rice. Cook rice according to package directions. Serve gumbo over rice. Sprinkle with chopped parsley, if desired.

Makes 4 servings

Note: If gumbo thickens upon standing, stir in additional broth.

Smoked Sausage Gumbo

Easy Beefy Sandwiches

1 (2- to 4-pound) beef rump roast
1 package (1 ounce) Italian salad dressing mix
1 package (1 ounce) dried onion soup mix
2 beef bouillon cubes
2 tablespoons prepared yellow mustard
  Garlic powder
  Onion powder
  Salt
  Black pepper
1 to 1½ cups water

SLOW COOKER DIRECTIONS
Place roast, salad dressing mix, onion soup mix, bouillon cubes and mustard in slow cooker. Season to taste with garlic powder, onion powder, salt and pepper. Add enough water to cover roast. Cover and cook on LOW 8 to 10 hours.   *Makes 6 to 8 servings*

Serving Suggestion: Slice roast and serve with provolone, mozzarella or Swiss cheese on hard rolls.

To adapt your own recipes to slow cooking, reduce the liquid by about one half, and add dairy products toward the end of the cooking time. Check similar recipes for an approximate cooking time. Taste the dish near the end of the cooking period and adjust seasonings, if necessary.

Easy Beefy Sandwich

Classic Cabbage Rolls

6 cups water
12 large cabbage leaves
1 pound lean ground lamb
½ cup cooked rice
1 teaspoon salt
¼ teaspoon dried oregano leaves
¼ teaspoon ground nutmeg
¼ teaspoon black pepper
1½ cups tomato sauce

SLOW COOKER DIRECTIONS

Bring water to a boil in large saucepan. Turn off heat. Soak cabbage leaves in water 5 minutes; remove, drain and cool.

Combine lamb, rice, salt, oregano, nutmeg and pepper in large bowl; mix until well blended. Place 2 tablespoonfuls mixture in center of each cabbage leaf; roll firmly. Place cabbage rolls in slow cooker, seam side down. Pour tomato sauce over cabbage rolls. Cover and cook on LOW 8 to 10 hours.   *Makes 6 servings*

102

Helpful Hint

For best results when making stuffed cabbage rolls, look for a cabbage head with large, dark green leaves loosely attached. For this recipe, two heads of cabbage may be needed to get enough leaves.

Classic Cabbage Rolls

Hamburger Soup

1 pound lean ground beef
1 package (1 ounce) dried onion soup mix
1 package (1 ounce) Italian seasoning mix
¼ teaspoon seasoned salt
¼ teaspoon black pepper
3 cups boiling water
1 can (8 ounces) diced tomatoes, undrained
1 can (8 ounces) tomato sauce
1 tablespoon soy sauce
1 cup sliced celery
1 cup thinly sliced carrots
2 cups cooked macaroni
¼ cup grated Parmesan cheese
2 tablespoons chopped fresh parsley

SLOW COOKER DIRECTIONS

1. Brown beef in medium skillet over medium-high heat; drain. Add beef to slow cooker. Add soup mix, Italian seasoning, seasoned salt and pepper. Stir in water, tomatoes with juice, tomato sauce and soy sauce. Add celery and carrots. Cover and cook on LOW 6 to 8 hours.

2. Increase to HIGH; stir in cooked macaroni and Parmesan cheese. Cover and cook 10 to 15 minutes until heated through. Sprinkle with parsley just before serving.

Makes 6 to 8 servings

104

Helpful Hint

Browning ground beef before placing it in the slow cooker, gives the beef a more attractive color and a richer flavor. Always be sure to drain off excess grease, thus reducing the amount of fat in the finished recipe.

Hamburger Soup

Fiesta Rice and Sausage

1 teaspoon vegetable oil
2 pounds spicy Italian sausage, casing removed
2 cloves garlic, minced
2 teaspoons ground cumin
4 onions, chopped
4 green bell peppers, chopped
3 jalapeño peppers,* seeded and minced
4 cups beef broth
2 packages (6¼ ounces each) long-grain and wild rice mix

*Jalapeño peppers can sting and irritate the skin; wear rubber gloves when handling peppers and do not touch eyes. Wash hands after handling peppers.

SLOW COOKER DIRECTIONS
Heat oil in large skillet over medium-high heat; cook sausage until no longer pink, stirring to separate meat. Add garlic and cumin; cook 30 seconds. Add onions, bell peppers and jalapeño peppers. Cook and stir until onions are tender, about 10 minutes. Pour mixture into slow cooker. Stir in beef broth and rice mix.

Cover and cook on HIGH 1 to 2 hours or on LOW 4 to 6 hours. *Makes 10 to 12 servings*

106

For a less spicy dish, reduce the number of jalapeño peppers and be sure to remove the white membranes and the seeds attached to them.

Fiesta Rice and Sausage

Sausage, Butter Bean and Cabbage Soup

  2 tablespoons butter, divided
  1 large onion, chopped
12 ounces smoked sausage such as kielbasa or andouille, cut into ½-inch slices
  8 cups chicken broth
  3 tablespoons tomato paste
½ savoy cabbage, coarsely shredded
  1 bay leaf
  4 medium tomatoes, chopped
  2 cans (14 ounces each) butter beans, drained
    Salt and black pepper, to taste

SLOW COOKER DIRECTIONS

1. Melt 1 tablespoon butter in large skillet over medium heat. Add onion; cook and stir 3 to 4 minutes or until golden. Place in slow cooker.

2. Melt remaining 1 tablespoon butter in the same skillet; cook sausage until brown on both sides. Add to slow cooker.

3. Place chicken broth, tomato paste, cabbage and bay leaf in slow cooker; stir until well blended. Cover; cook on LOW 4 hours or on HIGH 2 hours.

4. Add tomatoes and beans; season with salt and pepper. Cover; cook 1 hour until heated through. Remove and discard bay leaf. *Makes 6 servings*

Savoy cabbage, sometimes called curly cabbage, is a large, round cabbage with pale to dark green crinkled leaves. If savoy cabbage is unavailable, the more common green cabbage may be substituted.

Creamy Beef and Noodles

- **1 tablespoon vegetable oil**
- **2 pounds beef stew meat, cut into 1-inch pieces**
- **1 jar (4 ounces) sliced mushrooms, drained**
- **¼ cup minced onion**
- **3 cloves garlic, minced**
- **1 teaspoon salt**
- **1 teaspoon black pepper**
- **⅛ teaspoon dried thyme leaves**
- **1 bay leaf**
- **1 can (13¾ ounces) beef broth**
- **⅓ cup cooking sherry**
- **1 cup (8 ounces) sour cream**
- **½ cup all-purpose flour**
- **¼ cup water**
- **4 cups hot cooked noodles**

SLOW COOKER DIRECTIONS

109

Heat oil in large skillet over medium-high heat. Add beef; cook and stir until brown, stirring to separate meat. Drain off fat.

Place beef, mushrooms, onion, garlic, salt, pepper, thyme and bay leaf in slow cooker. Add beef broth and sherry. Cover and cook on LOW 8 to 10 hours. Remove and discard bay leaf.

Increase heat to HIGH. Combine sour cream, flour and water in small bowl. Stir about 1 cup of hot liquid into sour cream mixture. Stir mixture into slow cooker. Cover and cook on HIGH 30 minutes or until thickened and bubbly. Serve over noodles. *Makes 6 to 8 servings*

 *Helpful Hint*

Some seasonings like herbs and black pepper tend to mellow during long cooking in a slow cooker. Taste the dish just before serving and add more seasonings, if necessary.

Vegetable Pasta Sauce

2 cans (14½ ounces each) diced tomatoes, undrained
1 can (14½ ounces) whole tomatoes, undrained
1½ cups sliced mushrooms
1 medium red bell pepper, diced
1 medium green bell pepper, diced
1 small zucchini, cut into ¼-inch slices
1 small yellow squash, cut into ¼-inch slices
1 can (6 ounces) tomato paste
4 green onions, sliced
2 tablespoons dried Italian seasoning
1 tablespoon chopped fresh parsley
3 cloves garlic, minced
1 teaspoon salt
1 teaspoon red pepper flakes (optional)
1 teaspoon black pepper
Cooked pasta
Parmesan cheese and fresh basil for garnish (optional)

SLOW COOKER DIRECTIONS
Combine all ingredients except pasta and garnishes in slow cooker, stirring until well blended. Cover and cook on LOW 6 to 8 hours. Serve over cooked pasta. Garnish with Parmesan cheese and fresh basil, if desired.   *Makes 4 to 6 servings*

110

Vegetable Pasta Sauce

Mom's Tuna Casserole

2 cans (12 ounces each) tuna, drained and flaked
3 cups diced celery
3 cups crushed potato chips, divided
6 hard-cooked eggs, chopped
1 can (10¾ ounces) condensed cream of mushroom soup, undiluted
1 can (10¾ ounces) condensed cream of celery soup, undiluted
1 cup mayonnaise
1 teaspoon dried tarragon leaves
1 teaspoon black pepper

SLOW COOKER DIRECTIONS
Combine tuna, celery, 2½ cups potato chips, eggs, soups, mayonnaise, tarragon and pepper in slow cooker; stir until well blended. Sprinkle with remaining ½ cup potato chips. Cover and cook on LOW 5 to 8 hours.

Makes 8 servings

112

To hard cook eggs, place them in a single layer in a saucepan; cover them with cold water. Bring the water to a boil; remove the saucepan from the heat, cover and let the eggs stand for 15 minutes. Drain off the water and cover the eggs with cold water, replenishing it as needed until the eggs are cool.

Mom's Tuna Casserole

Shrimp Jambalaya

1 can (28 ounces) diced tomatoes, undrained
1 medium onion, chopped
1 medium red bell pepper, chopped
1 rib celery, chopped (about ½ cup)
2 tablespoons minced garlic
2 teaspoons dried parsley flakes
2 teaspoons dried oregano leaves
1 teaspoon red pepper sauce
½ teaspoon thyme leaves
2 pounds large peeled, deveined shrimp, cooked
2 cups uncooked instant rice
2 cups fat-free low-sodium chicken broth

SLOW COOKER DIRECTIONS
Combine tomatoes with juice, onion, bell pepper, celery, garlic, parsley, oregano, pepper sauce and thyme in slow cooker. Cover and cook on LOW 8 hours or on HIGH 4 hours. Stir in shrimp. Cover and cook on LOW 20 minutes.

Meanwhile, prepare rice according to package directions, substituting broth for water. Serve jambalaya over hot cooked rice.   *Makes 6 servings*

 *Helpful Hint*

To devein shrimp, make a small slit along the outer curve of the shrimp with a paring knife and remove the dark vein. This task is easier if it is done under cold, running water.

Southwest Bean Chili

1 can (16 ounces) tomato sauce
2 medium green bell peppers, seeded and chopped
1 can (15 ounces) garbanzo beans, rinsed and drained
1 can (15 ounces) red kidney beans, rinsed and drained
1 can (15 ounces) black beans, rinsed and drained
1 can (14½ ounces) Mexican-style stewed tomatoes, undrained
1½ cups frozen corn
1 cup chicken broth
3 tablespoons chili powder
4 cloves garlic, minced
1 tablespoon unsweetened cocoa powder
1 teaspoon ground cumin
½ teaspoon salt
Hot cooked rice

TOPPINGS
Shredded cheese, sliced ripe olives, avocado and green onion slices (optional)

SLOW COOKER DIRECTIONS
Combine all ingredients except rice and toppings in slow cooker; stir until well blended. Cover and cook on LOW 6 to 6½ hours or until vegetables are tender.

Spoon rice into bowls; top with chili. Serve with toppings, if desired.

Makes 8 to 10 servings

Adding a little cocoa powder to a Southwestern chili or sauce makes a richer dish without adding sweetness. Grated Mexican chocolate, which contains a little cinnamon, may be substituted.

115

Caribbean Shrimp with Rice

1 package (12 ounces) frozen shrimp, thawed
½ cup chicken broth
1 clove garlic, minced
1 teaspoon chili powder
½ teaspoon salt
½ teaspoon dried oregano leaves
1 cup frozen peas, thawed
½ cup diced tomatoes
2 cups cooked rice

SLOW COOKER DIRECTIONS
Combine shrimp, broth, garlic, chili powder, salt and oregano in slow cooker. Cover and cook on LOW 2 hours. Add peas and tomatoes. Cover and cook on LOW 5 minutes. Stir in rice. Cover and cook on LOW an additional 5 minutes. *Makes 4 servings*

116

Hearty Mushroom and Barley Soup

9 cups chicken broth
1 pound fresh mushrooms, sliced
1 large onion, chopped
2 carrots, chopped
2 ribs celery, chopped
½ cup pearled barley
½ ounce dried porcini mushrooms
3 cloves garlic, minced
1 teaspoon salt
½ teaspoon dried thyme leaves
½ teaspoon black pepper

SLOW COOKER DIRECTIONS
Combine all ingredients in slow cooker; stir until well blended. Cover and cook on LOW 4 to 6 hours or until barley is tender. *Makes 8 to 10 servings*

Caribbean Shrimp with Rice

Chicken Enchilada Skillet Casserole

1 bag (16 ounces) BIRDS EYE® frozen Farm Fresh Mixtures Broccoli, Corn & Red Peppers
1 package (1¼ ounces) taco seasoning mix
1 can (16 ounces) diced tomatoes, undrained
3 cups shredded cooked chicken
1 cup shredded Monterey Jack cheese
8 ounces tortilla chips

• In large skillet, combine vegetables, seasoning mix, tomatoes and chicken; bring to boil over medium-high heat.

• Cover; cook 4 minutes or until vegetables are cooked and mixture is heated through.

• Sprinkle with cheese; cover and cook 2 minutes more or until cheese is melted.

• Serve with chips.   *Makes 4 servings*

Birds Eye Idea: Here's a quick lunch item for kids. Cut up 4 cooked hot dogs; stir into 1 bag of prepared Birds Eye® Pasta Secrets White Cheddar.

Prep Time: 5 minutes
Cook Time: 10 minutes

Chicken Enchilada Skillet Casserole

Curried Turkey and Couscous Skillet

1 tablespoon vegetable or olive oil
1 small onion, chopped
2 cloves garlic, minced
1 can (10½ ounces) kosher condensed chicken broth
⅓ cup water
2 teaspoons curry powder
¼ teaspoon ground red pepper
2 cups small broccoli flowerets
1 cup thinly sliced carrots
2 packages (4 ounces each) HEBREW NATIONAL® Sliced Oven Roasted Turkey Breast, cut
     into ½-inch strips
1 cup uncooked couscous
     Chopped fresh cilantro, for garnish

Heat oil in large deep nonstick skillet over medium heat. Add onion and garlic; cook 5 minutes or until onion is tender. Add broth, water, curry powder and ground red pepper to skillet; bring to a boil. Stir in broccoli and carrots. Cover; simmer 5 minutes or until vegetables are crisp-tender.

Stir turkey into broth mixture; cook until heated through. Stir in couscous, mixing well. Cover; remove from heat. Let stand 5 minutes or until liquid is absorbed. Garnish with cilantro, if desired.

Makes 4 servings

120

Couscous is coarsely ground durum wheat. It is a staple in North African cuisines. Most couscous available in the United States is precooked, which means it requires little or no cooking.

Lemon-Garlic Chicken & Rice

4 skinless, boneless chicken breast halves
1 teaspoon paprika
  Salt and pepper (optional)
2 tablespoons margarine or butter
2 cloves garlic, minced
1 package (6.9 ounces) RICE-A-RONI® Chicken Flavor
1 tablespoon lemon juice
1 cup chopped red or green bell pepper
½ teaspoon grated lemon peel

1. Sprinkle chicken with paprika, salt and pepper.

2. In large skillet, melt margarine over medium-high heat. Add chicken and garlic; cook 2 minutes on each side or until browned. Remove from skillet; set aside, reserving drippings. Keep warm.

3. In same skillet, sauté rice-vermicelli mix in reserved drippings over medium heat until vermicelli is golden brown. Stir in 2¼ cups water, lemon juice and Special Seasonings. Top rice with chicken; bring to a boil over high heat.

4. Cover; reduce heat. Simmer 10 minutes. Stir in red pepper and lemon peel.

5. Cover; continue to simmer 10 minutes or until liquid is absorbed, rice is tender and chicken is no longer pink inside.

Makes 4 servings

Lemon-Garlic Chicken & Rice

Chicken Garden "Risotto"

2 boneless, skinless chicken breast halves
2 tablespoons CRISCO® Oil*
1 large sweet onion, finely chopped
1 tablespoon jarred minced garlic (or 2 large garlic cloves, peeled and minced)
1¾ cups (12 ounces) uncooked orzo pasta
2 cups broccoli flowerets, cut into bite-size pieces *or* 1 package (10½ ounces) frozen broccoli, thawed
2 cans (14½ ounces each) reduced-sodium chicken stock or broth
2 ears fresh corn, kernels cut from cobs *or* 1 package (10½ ounces) frozen corn, thawed
¼ teaspoon salt
¼ teaspoon freshly ground black pepper
¾ cup freshly grated Parmesan cheese

*Use your favorite Crisco Oil product.

1. Rinse chicken. Pat dry. Cut into 1-inch pieces.

2. Heat oil in 12-inch skillet on medium-high heat. Add onion and garlic. Cook 2 minutes. Add orzo, broccoli and broth. Reduce heat to medium. Cover skillet. Cook 6 minutes, stirring frequently. Add chicken. Cook 6 minutes. Mix in corn, salt and pepper. Cook 5 minutes.

3. Remove pan from heat. Stir in cheese gently. Serve hot. *Makes 4 to 6 servings*

Note: Any combination of vegetables can be used, such as fresh or frozen peas, sliced carrots, sliced mushrooms, sliced zucchini or yellow squash.

Preparation Time: 20 minutes
Total Time: 35 minutes

Quick Chicken Jambalaya

8 boneless, skinless chicken thighs, cut in bite-size pieces
¼ teaspoon garlic salt
1 tablespoon vegetable oil
2½ cups 8-vegetable juice
1 bag (16 ounces) frozen pepper stir-fry mix
½ cup diced cooked ham
1 teaspoon hot pepper sauce
1¾ cups quick-cooking rice, uncooked

Sprinkle garlic salt over chicken. In large nonstick skillet, place oil and heat to medium-high temperature. Add chicken and cook, stirring occasionally, 8 minutes or until chicken is lightly browned. Add vegetable juice, pepper stir-fry mix, ham and hot pepper sauce. Heat to boiling; cover and cook over medium heat 4 minutes. Stir in rice; heat to boiling. Cover, remove pan from heat and let stand 5 minutes or until rice and vegetables are tender and liquid is absorbed. *Makes 4 servings*

*Favorite recipe from **Delmarva Poultry Industry, Inc.***

125

Italian-Style Chicken and Rice

1 tablespoon vegetable oil
4 boneless skinless chicken breasts (about 1 pound)
2 cups reduced-sodium chicken broth
1 box (about 6 ounces) chicken-flavored rice mix
½ cup chopped red bell pepper
½ cup frozen peas, thawed
¼ cup grated Romano cheese

1. Heat oil in large skillet. Add chicken; cook over medium high heat 10 to 15 minutes or until lightly browned on both sides.

2. Add broth, rice mix, bell pepper and peas; mix well. Bring to a boil. Cover; reduce heat and simmer 10 minutes or until chicken is no longer pink in center. Remove from heat. Sprinkle with cheese, let stand covered 5 minutes or until liquid is absorbed. *Makes 4 servings*

Creole Chicken Thighs & Rice

2 tablespoons vegetable oil
2¼ pounds chicken thighs
½ teaspoon paprika
½ teaspoon dried thyme leaves
½ teaspoon salt
¼ teaspoon black pepper
½ cup chopped celery
½ cup chopped green bell pepper
½ cup chopped onion
2 cloves garlic, minced
1 cup long-grain or converted rice
1 can (14½ ounces) diced tomatoes, undrained
1 cup water
 Hot pepper sauce, to taste

Heat oil in large skillet or Dutch oven over medium heat until hot. Sprinkle chicken with paprika, thyme, salt and black pepper. Cook chicken 5 to 6 minutes on each side or until golden brown. Remove from skillet.

Add celery, bell pepper, onion and garlic to same skillet; cook 2 minutes. Add rice; cook 2 minutes, stirring to coat rice with oil. Stir in tomatoes with juice and water. Season with hot pepper sauce; bring to a boil.

Arrange chicken over rice mixture; reduce heat. Cover; simmer 20 minutes or until chicken is no longer pink in center and liquid is absorbed. *Makes 4 servings*

Creole Chicken Thighs & Rice

Northwoods Mushroom Swiss Melt

4 TYSON® Individually Fresh Frozen® Boneless, Skinless Chicken Breasts
2 boxes UNCLE BEN'S® Long Grain & Wild Rice Original Recipe
3¾ cups water
½ cup chopped green bell pepper
½ cup chopped red bell pepper
1 cup sliced mushrooms
4 slices Swiss cheese

COOK: CLEAN: Wash hands. Remove protective ice glaze from frozen chicken by holding under cool running water 1 to 2 minutes. Spray large skillet with nonstick cooking spray. Add chicken; cook over medium-high heat 5 to 7 minutes or until light brown. Add water, rice and contents of seasoning packets. Bring to a boil. Cover, reduce heat; simmer 20 minutes. Stir in bell peppers; sprinkle mushrooms over chicken. Cook, covered, 5 to 8 minutes or until internal juices of chicken run clear. (Or insert instant-read meat thermometer in thickest part of chicken. Temperature should read 170°F.) Place cheese over chicken; remove from heat. Let stand, covered, 5 minutes or until cheese is melted.

SERVE: Serve chicken while still hot with rolls and mixed vegetables, if desired.

CHILL: Refrigerate leftovers immediately.   *Makes 4 servings*

Prep Time: none
Cook Time: 40 minutes

128

Simmered Tuscan Chicken

2 tablespoons olive or vegetable oil
1 pound boneless, skinless chicken breasts, cut into 1-inch cubes
2 cloves garlic, finely chopped
4 medium potatoes, cut into ½-inch cubes (about 4 cups)
1 medium red bell pepper, cut into large pieces
1 jar (26 to 28 ounces) RAGÚ® Old World Style® Pasta Sauce
1 pound fresh or frozen cut green beans
1 teaspoon dried basil leaves, crushed
Salt and ground black pepper to taste

In 12-inch skillet, heat oil over medium-high heat and cook chicken with garlic until chicken is no longer pink. Remove chicken and set aside.

In same skillet, add potatoes and bell pepper. Cook over medium heat, stirring occasionally, 5 minutes. Stir in remaining ingredients. Bring to a boil over high heat. Reduce heat to low and simmer covered, stirring occasionally, 35 minutes or until potatoes are tender. Return chicken to skillet and heat through.   *Makes 6 servings*

Simmered Tuscan Chicken

Jiffy Chicken Supper

1 bag (16 ounces) BIRDS EYE® frozen Pasta Secrets White Cheddar or Creamy Peppercorn
¼ cup water
1 can (6½ ounces) chicken, drained
¼ cup pitted ripe olives, sliced
1 cup (8 ounces) plain yogurt
2 tablespoons chopped fresh parsley

● In large skillet, place Pasta Secrets and water. Bring to boil over high heat. Reduce heat to medium; cover and simmer 7 to 9 minutes or until pasta is tender.

● Stir in chicken and olives; cook 5 minutes more.

● In small bowl, combine yogurt and parsley.

● Stir yogurt mixture into Pasta Secrets mixture; cover and cook over low heat 1 minute or until heated through. *Makes 4 servings*

Birds Eye Idea: To get a quick topping of crumbs for casseroles or skillets, rub two slices of toast together directly over the top. The crumbs will fall like magic!

Prep Time: 5 minutes
Cook Time: 15 to 18 minutes

132

Skillet Chicken Pot Pie

1 can (10¾ ounces) reduced-sodium cream of chicken soup
1¼ cups fat-free (skim) milk, divided
1 package (10 ounces) frozen mixed vegetables
2 cups diced cooked chicken
½ teaspoon black pepper
1 cup buttermilk biscuit baking mix
¼ teaspoon summer savory or parsley

1. Heat soup, 1 cup milk, vegetables, chicken and pepper in medium skillet over medium heat until mixture comes to a boil.

2. Meanwhile, combine biscuit mix and summer savory in small bowl. Stir in remaining 3 to 4 tablespoons milk just until soft batter is formed. Drop batter by tablespoonfuls onto chicken mixture to make 6 dumplings. Partially cover and simmer 12 minutes or until dumplings are cooked through, spooning liquid from pot pie over dumplings once or twice during cooking. Garnish with additional summer savory, if desired. *Makes 6 servings*

Prep and Cook Time: 25 minutes

One-Pot Chicken Couscous

    2 pounds boneless, skinless chicken breasts, cut into 1-inch chunks
    ¼ cup olive oil
    4 large carrots, peeled and sliced
    2 medium onions, diced
    2 large cloves garlic, minced
    2 cans (13¾ ounces each) chicken broth
    2 cups uncooked couscous
    2 teaspoons TABASCO® brand Pepper Sauce
    ½ teaspoon salt
    1 cup raisins or currants
    1 cup slivered almonds, toasted
    ¼ cup chopped fresh parsley or mint

Cook chicken in hot oil in 12-inch skillet over medium-high heat until well browned on all sides. With slotted spoon, remove chicken to plate. Reduce heat to medium. In remaining drippings cook carrots and onions 5 minutes. Add garlic; cook 2 minutes longer, stirring frequently.

Add chicken broth, couscous, TABASCO® Sauce, salt and chicken chunks. Heat to boiling, then reduce heat to low. Cover and simmer 5 minutes. Stir in raisins, almonds and parsley.

Makes 8 servings

133

Southern BBQ Chicken and Rice

1 cup UNCLE BEN'S® ORIGINAL CONVERTED® Brand Rice
4 TYSON® Individually Fresh Frozen® Chicken Half Breasts
1½ cups water
1 cup barbecue sauce, divided
1 package (6 half ears) frozen corn on the cob

COOK: CLEAN: Wash hands. In large skillet, combine water, rice, ¾ cup barbecue sauce and chicken. Bring to a boil. Cover, reduce heat; simmer 25 minutes. Add corn; cook 15 to 20 minutes or until internal juices of chicken run clear. (Or insert instant-read meat thermometer in thickest part of chicken. Temperature should read 170°F.) Spoon remaining ¼ cup barbecue sauce over chicken. Remove from heat; let stand 5 minutes or until liquid is absorbed.

SERVE: Serve with extra barbecue sauce and corn bread, if desired.

CHILL: Refrigerate leftovers immediately.

Makes 4 servings

134

Prep Time: none
Cook Time: 40 to 45 minutes

Skillet meals are ideal, easy-to-prepare recipes that include protein, starch and vegetables—an entire meal in one skillet. Cleanup is quick, too!

Curried Chicken with Couscous

1 package (5.7 ounces) curry flavor couscous mix
1 tablespoon butter or margarine
1 pound boneless skinless chicken breasts, cut into thin strips
½ bag (16 ounces) BIRDS EYE® frozen Farm Fresh Mixtures Broccoli, Cauliflower & Red Peppers
1⅓ cups water
½ cup raisins

- Remove seasoning packet from couscous mix; set aside.

- In large nonstick skillet, melt butter over medium-high heat. Add chicken; cook until browned on all sides.

- Stir in vegetables, water, raisins and seasoning packet; bring to boil. Reduce heat to medium-low; cover and simmer 5 minutes or until chicken is no longer pink in center.

- Stir in couscous; cover. Remove from heat; let stand 5 minutes. Stir before serving.

Makes 4 servings

136

Serving Suggestion: Serve with toasted pita bread rounds.

Birds Eye Idea: To add flavor to chicken breasts, simply rub them with lemon juice before cooking.

Prep Time: 5 minutes
Cook Time: 15 minutes

Curried Chicken with Couscous

Potato and Pork Frittata

12 ounces (about 3 cups) frozen hash brown potatoes
1 teaspoon Cajun seasoning
4 egg whites
2 whole eggs
¼ cup low-fat (1%) milk
1 teaspoon dry mustard
¼ teaspoon black pepper
10 ounces (about 3 cups) frozen stir-fry vegetable blend
⅓ cup water
¾ cup chopped cooked lean pork
½ cup (2 ounces) shredded Cheddar cheese

1. Preheat oven to 400°F. Spray baking sheet with nonstick cooking spray. Spread potatoes on baking sheet; sprinkle with Cajun seasoning. Bake 15 minutes or until hot. Remove from oven. *Reduce oven temperature to 350°F.*

2. Beat egg whites, eggs, milk, mustard and pepper in small bowl. Place vegetables and water in medium ovenproof nonstick skillet. Cook over medium heat 5 minutes or until vegetables are crisp-tender; drain.

3. Add pork and potatoes to vegetables in skillet; stir lightly. Add egg mixture. Sprinkle with cheese. Cook over medium-low heat 5 minutes. Place skillet in 350°F oven and bake 5 minutes or until egg mixture is set and cheese is melted. *Makes 4 servings*

Prep and Cook Time: 30 minutes

Helpful Hint

Two whole eggs may be substituted for the four egg whites, if desired.

Potato and Pork Frittata

138

Velveeta® Cheeseburger Mac

1 pound ground beef
2¾ cups water
⅓ cup catsup
1 to 2 teaspoons onion powder
2 cups (8 ounces) elbow macaroni, uncooked
¾ pound (12 ounces) VELVEETA® Pasteurized Prepared Cheese Product, cut up

1. Brown meat in large skillet; drain.

2. Stir in water, catsup and onion powder. Bring to boil. Stir in macaroni. Reduce heat to medium-low; cover. Simmer 8 to 10 minutes or until macaroni is tender.

3. Add Velveeta; stir until melted.   *Makes 4 to 6 servings*

Safe Food Handling: Store ground beef in the coldest part of the refrigerator for up to 2 days. Make sure raw juices do not touch other foods. Ground meat can be wrapped airtight and frozen for up to 3 months.

140

Prep Time: 10 minutes
Cook Time: 15 minutes

French-American Rice

½ pound lean ground beef or ground turkey
1 box (10 ounces) BIRDS EYE® frozen White and Wild Rice
1½ teaspoons soy sauce
½ cup California walnuts

• In large skillet, cook beef over medium-high heat 5 minutes or until well browned.

• Stir in rice; cook 5 minutes more or until rice is tender, stirring occasionally.

• Stir in soy sauce and California walnuts; cook 1 minute or until heated.

Makes 4 servings

Prep Time: 5 minutes
Cook Time: 10 minutes

Velveeta® Cheeseburger Mac

Pork Chops with Apples and Stuffing

4 pork chops, ½ inch thick
  Salt and pepper
1 tablespoon oil
2 medium apples, cored, cut into 8 wedges
1 cup apple juice
2 cups STOVE TOP® Cornbread Stuffing Mix in the Canister
¼ cup chopped pecans

SPRINKLE chops with salt and pepper. Heat oil in large skillet on medium-high heat. Add chops and apples; cook until chops are browned on both sides.

STIR in apple juice. Bring to a boil. Reduce heat to low; cover and simmer 8 minutes or until chops are cooked through. Remove chops from skillet.

STIR Stuffing Mix Pouch and pecans into skillet. Return chops to skillet; cover. Remove from heat. Let stand 5 minutes.   *Makes 4 servings*

142

Prep Time: 10 minutes
Cook Time: 20 minutes

Skillet Franks and Potatoes

3 tablespoons vegetable oil, divided
4 HEBREW NATIONAL® Quarter Pound Dinner Beef Franks or 4 Beef Knockwurst
3 cups chopped cooked red potatoes
1 cup chopped onion
1 cup chopped seeded green bell pepper or combination of green and red bell peppers
3 tablespoons chopped fresh parsley (optional)
1 teaspoon dried sage leaves
½ teaspoon salt
¼ teaspoon freshly ground black pepper

Heat 1 tablespoon oil in large nonstick skillet over medium heat. Score franks; add to skillet. Cook franks until browned. Transfer to plate; set aside.

Add remaining 2 tablespoons oil to skillet. Add potatoes, onion and bell pepper; cook and stir about 12 to 14 minutes or until potatoes are golden brown. Stir in parsley, sage, salt and black pepper.

Return franks to skillet; push down into potato mixture. Cook about 5 minutes or until heated through, turning once halfway through cooking time. *Makes 4 servings*

Spanish Rice and Meatballs

6 slices bacon
1 pound lean ground beef
½ cup soft bread crumbs
1 egg, slightly beaten
½ teaspoon salt
⅛ teaspoon black pepper
½ cup chopped onion
½ cup sliced celery
⅔ cup uncooked white rice
1½ cups water
1 can (14½ ounces) whole peeled tomatoes, cut into bite-size pieces
⅓ cup HEINZ® 57 Sauce
¼ teaspoon black pepper
⅛ teaspoon hot pepper sauce
1 green bell pepper, cut into ¾-inch chunks

In large skillet, cook bacon until crisp; remove, coarsely crumble and set aside. Drain drippings, reserving 1 tablespoon. In large bowl, combine beef, bread crumbs, egg, salt and ⅛ teaspoon black pepper. Form into 20 meatballs, using a rounded tablespoon for each. In same skillet, brown meatballs in reserved drippings; remove. In same skillet, sauté onion and celery until tender-crisp; drain excess fat. Add rice, water, tomatoes, 57 Sauce, ¼ teaspoon black pepper and hot pepper sauce. Cover; simmer 20 minutes. Stir in bacon, meatballs and bell pepper. Cover; simmer an additional 10 minutes or until rice is tender and liquid is absorbed, stirring occasionally. *Makes 4 servings (4 cups rice mixture)*

Sausage Ham Jambalaya

6 ounces spicy smoked sausage links, sliced
6 ounces cooked ham, diced
2 cans (14½ ounces each) DEL MONTE® Original Recipe Stewed Tomatoes
1 cup uncooked long grain white rice
1 large clove garlic, minced
1 tablespoon chopped fresh parsley
1 bay leaf

1. Brown sausage and ham in heavy 4-quart saucepan. Drain tomatoes, reserving liquid; pour liquid into measuring cup. Add water to measure 1½ cups.

2. Add reserved liquid, tomatoes and remaining ingredients to sausage mixture.

3. Cover and simmer 30 to 35 minutes, stirring occasionally. Remove bay leaf. Garnish with additional chopped parsley, if desired.   *Makes 4 to 6 servings*

Prep Time: 10 minutes
Cook Time: 40 minutes

144

Beef Sonoma & Rice

1 pound lean ground beef (80% lean)
1 clove garlic, minced
1 package (6.8 ounces) RICE-A-RONI® Beef Flavor
½ cup chopped green bell pepper *or* 1 can (4 ounces) chopped green chiles, undrained
¼ cup sliced green onions
1 medium tomato, chopped
2 tablespoons chopped parsley or cilantro

1. In large skillet, brown ground beef and garlic; drain. Remove from skillet; set aside.

2. In same skillet, prepare Rice-A-Roni Mix as package directs, stirring in beef mixture, green pepper and onions during last 5 minutes of cooking.

3. Sprinkle with tomato and parsley.   *Makes 4 servings*

Sausage Ham Jambalaya

Taco Pot Pie

1 pound ground beef
1 package (1¼ ounces) taco seasoning mix
¼ cup water
1 can (8 ounces) kidney beans, rinsed and drained
1 cup chopped tomato
¾ cup frozen corn, thawed
¾ cup frozen peas, thawed
1½ cups (6 ounces) shredded Cheddar cheese
1 can (11½ ounces) refrigerated corn breadstick dough

1. Preheat oven to 400°F. Brown meat in medium ovenproof skillet over medium-high heat, stirring to separate; drain drippings. Add seasoning mix and water to skillet. Cook over medium-low heat 3 minutes or until most of liquid is absorbed, stirring occasionally.

2. Stir in beans, tomato, corn and peas. Cook 3 minutes or until mixture is hot. Remove from heat; stir in cheese.

3. Unwrap corn bread dough; separate into 16 strips. Twist strips, cutting to fit skillet. Arrange attractively over meat mixture. Press ends of dough lightly to edge of skillet to secure. Bake 15 minutes or until corn bread is golden brown and meat mixture is bubbly.

Makes 4 to 6 servings

Prep and Cook Time: 30 minutes

146

Taco Pot Pie

New Orleans Rice and Sausage

½ **pound smoked sausage,* cut into slices**
1 **can (14½ ounces) stewed tomatoes, Cajun- or Italian-style**
¾ **cup water**
1¾ **cups uncooked instant rice**
   Dash TABASCO® Pepper Sauce or to taste
1 **bag (16 ounces) BIRDS EYE® frozen Farm Fresh Mixtures Broccoli, Corn and Red Peppers**

*For a spicy dish, use andouille sausage. Any type of kielbasa or turkey kielbasa can also be used.

Heat sausage in large skillet 2 to 3 minutes.

Add tomatoes, water, rice and TABASCO® Pepper Sauce; mix well.

Add vegetables; mix well. Cover and cook over medium heat 5 to 7 minutes or until rice is tender and vegetables are heated through.   *Makes 6 servings*

Prep Time: 5 minutes
Cook Time: 10 minutes

148

Creamy Pasta Primavera

1 **bag (16 ounces) BIRDS EYE® frozen Pasta Secrets Primavera**
½ **cup 1% milk**
2 **packages (3 ounces each) cream cheese, cubed**
1 **cup cubed ham**
¼ **cup grated Parmesan cheese**

• In large skillet, heat Pasta Secrets in milk over medium heat to a simmer; cover and simmer 7 to 9 minutes or until vegetables are tender.

• Add cream cheese; reduce heat to low and cook until cream cheese is melted, stirring often.

• Stir in ham and cheese; cover and cook 5 minutes more.   *Makes 4 servings*

Prep Time: 10 minutes
Cook Time: 20 minutes

New Orleans Rice and Sausage

Velveeta® Cheesy Beef Stroganoff

1 pound ground beef
2 cups water
3 cups (6 ounces) medium egg noodles, uncooked
¾ pound (12 ounces) VELVEETA® Pasteurized Prepared Cheese Product, cut up
1 can (10¾ ounces) condensed cream of mushroom soup
¼ teaspoon black pepper

1. Brown meat in large skillet; drain.

2. Stir in water. Bring to boil. Stir in noodles. Reduce heat to medium-low; cover. Simmer 8 minutes or until noodles are tender.

3. Add Velveeta, soup and pepper; stir until Velveeta is melted.   *Makes 4 to 6 servings*

Prep Time: 10 minutes
Cook Time: 15 minutes

150

Velveeta® 15 Minute Cheesy Rice with Ham & Broccoli

2 cups cooked ham cut into strips
2 cups fresh or frozen broccoli flowerets, thawed
1 cup water
1½ cups MINUTE® White Rice, uncooked
½ pound (8 ounces) VELVEETA® Pasteurized Prepared Cheese Product, cut up

1. Bring ham, broccoli and water to boil in large skillet. Cover. Cook on medium heat 3 minutes.

2. Stir in rice and Velveeta; cover. Remove from heat. Let stand 7 minutes. Stir until Velveeta is melted.   *Makes 4 servings*

Velveeta® Cheesy Beef Stroganoff

Skillet Spaghetti and Sausage

  ¼ **pound mild or hot Italian sausage links, sliced**
  ½ **pound ground beef**
  ¼ **teaspoon dried oregano, crushed**
  4 **ounces spaghetti, broken in half**
  1 **can (14½ ounces) DEL MONTE® Diced Tomatoes with Basil, Garlic & Oregano**
  1 **can (8 ounces) DEL MONTE Tomato Sauce**
1½ **cups sliced fresh mushrooms**
  2 **stalks celery, sliced**

1. Brown sausage in large skillet over medium-high heat. Add beef and oregano; season to taste with salt and pepper, if desired.

2. Cook, stirring occasionally, until beef is browned; drain.

3. Add pasta, 1 cup water, undrained tomatoes, tomato sauce, mushrooms and celery. Bring to boil, stirring occasionally.

4. Reduce heat; cover and simmer 12 to 14 minutes or until spaghetti is tender. Garnish with grated Parmesan cheese and chopped parsley, if desired. Serve immediately.

Makes 4 to 6 servings

Prep Time: 5 minutes
Cook Time: 30 minutes

Easy Beef Stroganoff

  2 **tablespoons oil**
  2 **teaspoons finely chopped garlic**
  ½ **pound boneless sirloin steak, cut into thin strips**
  ¼ **cup dry red wine**
  2 **teaspoons Worcestershire sauce**
1¼ **cups water**
  ½ **cup milk**
  2 **tablespoons I CAN'T BELIEVE IT'S NOT BUTTER!® Spread**
  1 **package LIPTON® Noodles & Sauce—Stroganoff**
  ½ **cup peeled pearl onions**

In 12-inch skillet, heat oil over medium heat and cook garlic 30 seconds. Add beef and cook over medium-high heat 1 minute or until almost done. Add wine and Worcestershire sauce and cook 30 seconds; remove beef.

Into skillet, stir water, milk, I Can't Believe It's Not Butter!® Spread and Noodles & Sauce—Stroganoff. Bring to the boiling point, then continue boiling, stirring occasionally, 7 minutes. Stir in onions and beef, then cook 2 minutes or until noodles are tender. Garnish, if desired, with chopped parsley and paprika.   *Makes about 2 servings*

Note: Recipe is also delicious with Lipton® Noodles & Sauce—Beef Flavor.

Easy Beef and Rice Stew

    2 tablespoons flour
    ½ teaspoon salt
    ¼ teaspoon pepper
    1 pound boneless beef top round, cut into ¾-inch chunks
    1 tablespoon oil
    2 medium carrots, diagonally sliced
    1 medium onion, coarsely chopped
    1 jar (4½ ounces) sliced mushrooms, drained
    1 can (14½ ounces) whole tomatoes, undrained, coarsely chopped
    1 can (10¼ ounces) beef gravy
    ¼ cup burgundy or other dry red wine
 1½ cups MINUTE® Original Rice, uncooked

MIX flour, salt and pepper in large bowl. Add meat; toss to coat.

HEAT oil in large skillet on medium-high heat. Add meat; cook and stir until browned. Add carrots, onion and mushrooms; cook and stir 2 minutes.

STIR in tomatoes, gravy and wine. Bring to a boil. Reduce heat to low; cover and simmer 10 minutes.

STIR in rice; cover. Remove from heat. Let stand 5 minutes. Stir.   *Makes 4 servings*

Prep Time: 10 minutes
Cook Time: 20 minutes

153

Skillet Sausage and Bean Stew

1 pound spicy Italian sausage, casing removed and sliced into ½-inch slices
½ onion, chopped
2 cups frozen O'Brien-style potatoes with onions and peppers
1 can (15 ounces) pinto beans, undrained
1 teaspoon beef bouillon granules *or* 1 beef bouillon cube
1 teaspoon dried oregano leaves
⅛ teaspoon ground red pepper

1. Combine sausage slices and onion in large nonstick skillet; cook and stir over medium-high heat 5 to 7 minutes or until meat is no longer pink. Drain drippings.

2. Stir in potatoes, beans, ¾ cup water, bouillon, oregano and red pepper; reduce heat to medium. Cover and simmer 15 minutes, stirring occasionally. *Makes 4 servings*

154

Skillet Sausage and Peppers

1 pound bulk Italian sausage
1 medium onion, cut into wedges
1 small green pepper, cut into strips
1 small red pepper, cut into strips
1 can (8 ounces) tomato sauce
1 can (8 ounces) whole tomatoes, undrained
½ teaspoon dried oregano leaves
2 cups STOVE TOP® Chicken Flavor Stuffing Mix in the Canister

BROWN sausage in large skillet on medium-high heat. Stir in onion, peppers, tomato sauce, tomatoes and oregano. Bring to boil. Reduce heat to low; cover and simmer 5 minutes or until vegetables are tender-crisp.

STIR in Stuffing Mix Pouch just to moisten; cover. Remove from heat. Let stand 5 minutes.
Makes 4 servings

Prep Time: 15 minutes
Cook Time: 15 minutes

Skillet Sausage and Bean Stew

Steak Hash

2 tablespoons vegetable oil
1 green bell pepper, chopped
½ medium onion, chopped
1 pound russet potatoes, baked and chopped
8 ounces cooked steak or roast beef, cut into 1-inch cubes
Salt and black pepper, to taste
¼ cup (1 ounce) shredded Monterey Jack cheese
4 eggs

1. Heat oil in medium skillet over medium heat. Add bell pepper and onion; cook until tender. Stir in potatoes; reduce heat to low. Cover and cook, stirring occasionally, about 10 minutes or until potatoes are hot.

2. Stir in steak; season with salt and pepper. Sprinkle with cheese. Cover; cook about 5 minutes or until steak is hot and cheese is melted. Spoon onto 4 plates.

3. Meanwhile, prepare eggs as desired; top each serving with 1 egg.   *Makes 4 servings*

Chili with Rice

1 pound lean ground beef
2 cups water
1 can (15½ ounces) kidney beans, undrained
1 can (15 ounces) tomato sauce
1 package (1¾ ounces) chili seasoning mix
2 cups MINUTE® White Rice, uncooked
1 cup KRAFT® Shredded Cheddar Cheese

1. **BROWN** meat in large skillet on medium heat; drain.

2. **ADD** water, kidney beans, tomato sauce and seasoning mix. Bring to boil.

3. **STIR** in rice. Sprinkle with cheese; cover. Cook on low heat 5 minutes.   *Makes 6 servings*

Cook Time: 15 minutes

Steak Hash

Creamy Alfredo Seafood Newburg

2 tablespoons margarine or butter
¼ cup finely chopped onion
1 pound uncooked medium shrimp, peeled, deveined and coarsely chopped
1 jar (16 ounces) RAGÚ® Cheese Creations!® Classic Alfredo Sauce
¼ teaspoon ground white pepper
4 croissants or crescent rolls

1. In 12-inch nonstick skillet, melt margarine over medium-high heat and cook onion, stirring occasionally, 2 minutes or until tender.

2. Stir in shrimp and cook, stirring constantly, 2 minutes or until shrimp are almost pink. Stir in Ragú Cheese Creations! Sauce and pepper. Bring to a boil over high heat.

3. Reduce heat to low and simmer uncovered, stirring occasionally, 5 minutes or until shrimp turn pink. To serve, spoon shrimp mixture onto bottom of croissants and sprinkle, if desired, with chopped fresh parsley. Top with remaining croissant halves.   *Makes 4 servings*

Variation: For a light dish, substitute Ragú Cheese Creations! Light Parmesan Alfredo Sauce

Tip: Substitute 1 pound imitation crabmeat for shrimp.

Prep Time: 5 minutes
Cook Time: 15 minutes

Helpful Hint

This speedy version of Seafood Newburg is special enough to serve to dinner guests, but no one but you will know how easy it is to prepare.

Creamy Alfredo Seafood Newburg

Spicy Tuna and Linguine with Garlic and Pine Nuts

2 tablespoons olive oil
4 cloves garlic, minced
2 cups sliced mushrooms
½ cup chopped onion
½ teaspoon crushed red pepper
2½ cups chopped plum tomatoes
1 can (14½ ounces) chicken broth plus water to equal 2 cups
½ teaspoon salt
¼ teaspoon coarsely ground black pepper
1 package (9 ounces) uncooked fresh linguine
1 (7-ounce) pouch of STARKIST® Premium Albacore Tuna
⅓ cup chopped fresh cilantro
⅓ cup toasted pine nuts or almonds

In 12-inch skillet, heat olive oil over medium-high heat; sauté garlic, mushrooms, onion and red pepper until golden brown. Add tomatoes, chicken broth mixture, salt and black pepper; bring to a boil.

Separate uncooked linguine into strands; place in skillet and spoon sauce over. Reduce heat to simmer; cook, covered, 4 more minutes or until cooked through. Toss gently; add tuna and cilantro and toss again. Sprinkle with pine nuts. *Makes 4 to 6 servings*

Do you know?

Since the process to extract pine nuts from pine cones is labor intensive, these Mediterranean nuts are expensive. Also known as pignoli or pignolia, pine nuts contain a high percentage of oil. To prevent them from spoiling, store them in the refrigerator for up to 3 months or in the freezer for up to 9 months

*Spicy Tuna and Linguine with
Garlic and Pine Nuts*

Cheesy Deluxe Primavera Mac Skillet

2⅓ cups water
1 package (14 ounces) KRAFT® Light Deluxe Macaroni & Cheese Dinner
½ teaspoon dried basil leaves, crushed
½ teaspoon garlic powder
3 cups frozen vegetable medley (broccoli, cauliflower and carrots)

BRING water to boil in large skillet. Stir in Macaroni and seasonings; return to a boil.

STIR in vegetables. Reduce heat to medium-low; cover. Simmer 10 minutes or until macaroni is tender.

STIR in Cheese Sauce. Cook and stir 2 minutes on medium-high heat until thickened and creamy. *Makes 5 servings*

Prep Time: 5 minutes
Cook Time: 15 minutes

162

Creole Shrimp and Rice

2 tablespoons olive oil
1 cup uncooked white rice
1 can (15 ounces) diced tomatoes with garlic, undrained
1½ cups water
1 teaspoon Creole or Cajun seasoning blend
1 pound peeled cooked medium shrimp
1 package (10 ounces) frozen okra *or* 1½ cups frozen sugar snap peas, thawed

1. Heat oil in large skillet over medium heat until hot. Add rice; cook and stir 2 to 3 minutes or until lightly browned.

2. Add tomatoes with juice, water and seasoning blend; bring to a boil. Reduce heat; cover and simmer 15 minutes.

3. Add shrimp and okra. Cook, covered, 3 minutes or until heated through.
Makes 4 servings

Cheesy Deluxe Primavera Mac Skillet

Tuna Veronique

    2 leeks or green onions
½ cup thin carrot strips
    1 stalk celery, cut diagonally into slices
    1 tablespoon vegetable oil
1¾ cups *or* 1 can (14½ ounces) chicken broth
    2 tablespoons cornstarch
⅓ cup dry white wine
1¼ cups seedless red and green grapes, cut into halves
    1 (7-ounce) pouch of STARKIST® Premium Albacore or Chunk Light Tuna
    1 tablespoon chopped chives
¼ teaspoon ground white or black pepper
    4 to 5 slices bread, toasted and cut into quarters *or* 8 to 10 slices toasted French bread

If using leeks, wash thoroughly between leaves. Cut off white portion; trim and slice ¼ inch thick. Discard green portion. For green onions, trim and slice ¼ inch thick. In large nonstick skillet, sauté leeks, carrot and celery in oil for 3 minutes. In small bowl, stir together chicken broth and cornstarch until smooth; stir into vegetables. Cook and stir until mixture thickens and bubbles. Stir in wine; simmer 2 minutes. Stir in grapes, tuna, chives and pepper. Cook 2 minutes more to heat through. To serve, ladle sauce over toast.   *Makes 4 to 5 servings*

Prep Time: 20 minutes

Veronique is a French term used to describe dishes that include grapes as an ingredient or garnish.

Spicy Crabmeat Frittata

1 tablespoon olive oil
1 medium green bell pepper, finely chopped
2 cloves garlic, minced
6 eggs
1 can (6½ ounces) lump white crabmeat, drained
¼ teaspoon black pepper
¼ teaspoon salt
¼ teaspoon pepper sauce
1 large ripe plum tomato, seeded and finely chopped

1. Preheat broiler. Heat oil in 10-inch nonstick skillet with ovenproof handle over medium-high heat. Add bell pepper and garlic to skillet; cook and stir 3 minutes or until soft.

2. Meanwhile, beat eggs in medium bowl. Break up large pieces of crabmeat. Add crabmeat, black pepper, salt and pepper sauce to eggs; blend well. Set aside.

3. Add tomato to skillet, cook and stir for 1 minute. Add egg mixture. Reduce heat to medium-low; cook about 7 minutes or until eggs begin to set around edges.

165

4. Remove pan from burner and place under broiler 6 inches from heat. Broil about 2 minutes or until frittata is set and top is browned. Remove from broiler; slide frittata onto serving plate. Serve immediately.

Makes 4 servings

Tip: Serve with crusty bread, cut-up raw vegetables and guacamole.

Prep & Cook Time: 20 minutes

Fresh crabmeat may be substituted for the canned crabmeat in this frittata. Purchase fresh crabmeat the day you plan to use it; store it in the coldest part of the refrigerator until you are ready to use it.

Tempting Tuna Parmesano

2 large cloves garlic
1 package (9 ounces) refrigerated fresh angel hair pasta
¼ cup butter or margarine
1 cup whipping cream
1 cup frozen peas
¼ teaspoon salt
1 can (6 ounces) white tuna in water, drained
¼ cup grated Parmesan cheese, plus additional cheese for serving
Black pepper

1. Fill large deep skillet ¾ full with water. Cover and bring to a boil over high heat. Meanwhile, peel and mince garlic.

2. Add pasta to skillet; boil 1 to 2 minutes or until pasta is al dente. Do not overcook. Drain; set aside.

3. Add butter and garlic to skillet; cook over medium-high heat until butter is melted and sizzling. Stir in cream, peas and salt; bring to a boil.

4. Break tuna into chunks and stir into skillet with ¼ cup cheese. Return pasta to skillet. Cook until heated through; toss gently. Serve with additional cheese and pepper to taste.

Makes 2 to 3 servings

Serving Suggestion: Serve with a tossed romaine and tomato salad with Italian dressing.

Prep and Cook Time: 16 minutes

Tempting Tuna Parmesano

Thin Noodles with Chicken and Vegetables

6 ounces (about 3 cups) uncooked thin noodles or bean threads
½ cup chicken broth
2 tablespoons hoisin sauce
1 tablespoon vegetable oil
2 green onions, finely chopped
1 teaspoon minced fresh ginger
1 clove garlic, minced
1 pound boneless skinless chicken breasts, cut into bite-size pieces
1 package frozen vegetable medley,* thawed and drained
¼ cup orange marmalade
2 tablespoons chili sauce
¼ teaspoon red pepper flakes

*Use your favorite vegetable medley—for example, a medley of cauliflower, carrots and snow peas.

1. Place 6 cups water in wok or large saucepan; bring to a boil over high heat. Add noodles; cook 3 minutes or until *al dente,* stirring occasionally. Drain. Place noodles in medium bowl; stir in chicken broth and hoisin sauce. Set aside; keep warm.

2. Heat oil in wok or large skillet over high heat. Add onions, ginger and garlic; stir-fry 15 seconds. Add chicken; stir-fry 3 to 4 minutes. Add vegetables; stir-fry until vegetables are hot and chicken is no longer pink. Add marmalade, chili sauce and pepper flakes. Stir until hot. Serve over noodles.

Makes 4 servings

Get out the wok and stir-fry your way to a taste-tempting meal that just can't miss. Don't have a wok? That's okay, a large skillet will do.

Thin Noodles with Chicken and Vegetables

Chicken with Snow Peas

1½ **pounds boneless skinless chicken breasts, cut into bite-size pieces**
  3 **tablespoons light soy sauce**
  ¼ **cup all-purpose flour**
  2 **tablespoons sugar**
  1 **clove garlic, minced**
  ½ **teaspoon ground ginger**
  2 **tablespoons vegetable oil**
  4 **ounces shiitake or other fresh wild mushrooms, stemmed and cut into long thin strips**
  1 **red bell pepper, cut into 1-inch triangles**
  4 **ounces snow peas, trimmed**
1½ **cups chicken broth**
  1 **tablespoon cornstarch**
  ¼ **teaspoon black pepper**
     Hot cooked rice

1. Combine chicken and soy sauce in medium bowl; cover and refrigerate 15 minutes to 1 hour.

2. Combine flour, sugar, garlic and ginger in pie plate. Drain chicken, reserving marinade. Roll chicken in flour mixture.

3. Heat oil in wok or large skillet over high heat. Add chicken; stir-fry 3 to 4 minutes or until no longer pink.

4. Add mushrooms; stir-fry 1 minute. Add bell pepper and snow peas; stir-fry 1 to 2 minutes or until crisp-tender.

5. Whisk together reserved marinade, chicken broth, cornstarch and black pepper in small bowl; add to chicken mixture in wok. Cook and stir until sauce boils; boil 1 minute. Transfer to serving platter. Serve with rice. Garnish with kale leaves, if desired.

Makes 5 to 6 servings

Chicken with Snow Peas

Southwest Chicken and Beans

3 tablespoons lemon juice
2 tablespoons seasoned stir-fry or hot oil, divided
2 tablespoons finely chopped onion
1 tablespoon white wine vinegar
1 clove garlic, minced
2 teaspoons chili powder
1 teaspoon salt
½ teaspoon dried oregano leaves
½ teaspoon ground cumin
½ teaspoon black pepper
1 pound boneless skinless chicken breasts or tenders, cut into ¼-inch strips
1 medium red onion, cut into thin strips
2 large red bell peppers, cut into ¼-inch strips
1 tablespoon minced cilantro
2 cans (16 ounces each) refried beans, warmed
Tortilla chips, salsa and sour cream

1. Combine lemon juice, 1 tablespoon oil, chopped onion, vinegar, garlic, chili powder, salt, oregano, cumin and black pepper in medium bowl. Add chicken; toss to coat well. Cover and refrigerate 45 minutes to 8 hours.

2. Heat remaining 1 tablespoon oil in wok or large skillet over high heat. Add chicken mixture; stir-fry 3 minutes. Add onion strips; stir-fry 4 minutes. Add bell peppers; stir-fry 2 to 3 minutes or until vegetables are crisp-tender. Sprinkle with cilantro.

3. Serve chicken and vegetable mixture over beans with tortilla chips, salsa and sour cream on the side.   *Makes 4 to 5 servings*

Note: Seasoned stir-fry oils differ in "heat." If oil is too peppery, use 1 tablespoon vegetable oil and 1 tablespoon seasoned oil.

172

Southwest Chicken and Beans

Flash in the Pan Chicken & Veggie Stir-Fry

1½ pounds boneless skinless chicken, cut into 1-inch cubes
¼ cup teriyaki sauce
2 small zucchini, thinly sliced (about ¾ pound)
1 red or green bell pepper, cut into strips
1⅓ cups *French's*® French Fried Onions, divided
½ cup Italian salad dressing
1 teaspoon cornstarch

1. Toss chicken with teriyaki sauce. Heat 1 tablespoon oil in 12-inch nonstick skillet until hot. Stir-fry chicken 5 minutes or until browned. Add zucchini, pepper and ⅔ *cup* French Fried Onions; stir-fry 3 minutes or until vegetables are crisp-tender.

2. Combine dressing with cornstarch; stir into skillet. Heat to boiling. Cook 2 minutes or until sauce thickens. Sprinkle with remaining ⅔ *cup* onions.   *Makes 6 servings*

Prep Time: 10 minutes
Cook Time: 10 minutes

174

Quick Chicken Stir-Fry

½ cup MIRACLE WHIP® or MIRACLE WHIP LIGHT® Dressing, divided
4 boneless skinless chicken breast halves (about 1¼ pounds), cut into thin strips
¼ to ½ teaspoon garlic powder
1 package (16 ounces) frozen mixed vegetables *or* 3 cups fresh cut-up vegetables
2 tablespoons soy sauce
2 cups hot cooked MINUTE® White Rice

● Heat 2 tablespoons dressing in large skillet over medium-high heat. Add chicken and garlic powder; stir-fry 3 minutes.

● Add vegetables; stir-fry 3 minutes or until chicken is cooked through.

● Reduce heat to medium. Stir in remaining dressing and soy sauce; simmer 1 minute. Serve over rice.   *Makes 4 servings*

Prep Time: 10 minutes
Cook Time: 7 minutes

Stir-Fried Chicken with Broccoli

1 pound boneless skinless chicken tenders
2 tablespoons lemon juice
2 teaspoons grated lemon peel
1 teaspoon dried thyme leaves
½ teaspoon salt
¼ teaspoon ground white pepper
1 cup chicken broth
1 tablespoon cornstarch
3 tablespoons vegetable oil, divided
1 tablespoon butter
1 can (4 ounces) sliced mushrooms, drained
1 medium red onion, sliced
1 can (14 ounces) pre-cut baby corn*, rinsed and drained
2 cups frozen broccoli cuts, thawed
Hot cooked rice

*Or, substitute one (15-ounce) can whole baby corn, cut into 1-inch pieces.

1. Rinse chicken and pat dry with paper towels. Cut each chicken tender in half. Combine juice, lemon peel, thyme, salt and pepper in large bowl. Add chicken and toss to coat well. Marinate 10 minutes.

2. Stir broth into cornstarch in small bowl until smooth; set aside.

3. Heat wok over medium-high heat 1 minute or until hot. Drizzle 1 tablespoon oil into wok. Add butter and swirl to coat bottom; heat 30 seconds or until hot. Add mushrooms; stir-fry 1 minute. Add onion; stir-fry 2 minutes. Remove to large bowl.

4. Add remaining 2 tablespoons oil to wok and heat 1 minute or until hot. Add chicken in single layer; stir-fry 1½ minutes or until chicken is well browned on all sides and no longer pink in center. Remove to bowl with vegetable mixture.

5. Add corn to wok; stir-fry about 1 minute. Stir broth mixture until smooth; add to wok and cook until sauce boils and thickens. Add chicken mixture and broccoli; stir-fry until heated through. Serve over rice. *Makes 4 to 6 servings*

Note: Baby corn are tender miniature ears of corn that can be eaten cob and all. They're also great in soups and salads.

175

Oriental Chicken & Asparagus

6 TYSON® Fresh Boneless, Skinless Chicken Thighs
2 tablespoons cornstarch, divided
½ teaspoon salt
¼ pound fresh asparagus spears, trimmed and chopped
1 small red bell pepper, cut into thin strips
1 medium onion, sliced
2 tablespoons oyster sauce
1 clove garlic, minced
½ teaspoon sesame oil
1 can (14½ ounces) chicken broth
1 can (8 ounces) sliced water chestnuts, drained

PREP: CLEAN: Wash hands. Cut chicken into strips. CLEAN: Wash hands. Combine 1 tablespoon cornstarch and salt in medium bowl. Add chicken and stir to coat. Refrigerate.

COOK: Spray large nonstick skillet with nonstick cooking spray. Heat over medium-high heat. Cook and stir asparagus, bell pepper, onion, oyster sauce, garlic and oil about 3 minutes. Remove from pan. Cook and stir chicken about 5 minutes or until internal juices of chicken run clear. (Or insert instant-read meat thermometer in thickest part of chicken. Temperature should read 180°F.) Add broth and water chestnuts to skillet. Combine remaining 1 tablespoon cornstarch and ¼ cup water; add to skillet. Cook and stir until sauce is thickened. Return vegetables to skillet and heat through.

SERVE: Serve with cooked rice, if desired.

CHILL: Refrigerate leftovers immediately.

Makes 4 servings

Prep Time: 10 minutes
Cook Time: 20 minutes

Lemon Chicken Herb Stir-Fry

1 tablespoon plus 1½ teaspoons peanut oil
2 green onions, cut into 1-inch pieces
1 large carrot, julienne cut
4 boneless, skinless chicken breast halves (about 1 pound), cut into strips
2 cups broccoli flowerettes
1 can (8 ounces) bamboo shoots, drained
1 cup LAWRY'S® Herb & Garlic Marinade with Lemon Juice
1 tablespoon soy sauce
½ teaspoon arrowroot
1 can (11 ounces) mandarin orange segments, drained (optional)
1 tablespoon sesame seeds
3 cups hot cooked rice

In large wok or skillet, heat oil. Add onion and carrot and cook over medium-high heat 5 minutes. Add chicken, broccoli and bamboo shoots; stir-fry 7 to 9 minutes until chicken is no longer pink in center and juices run clear when cut. In small bowl, combine Herb & Garlic Marinade with Lemon Juice, soy sauce and arrowroot; mix well. Add to skillet; continue cooking, stirring constantly, until sauce forms glaze. Stir in orange segments. Sprinkle with sesame seeds. *Makes 6 servings*

Serving Suggestion: Serve over hot rice.

One pound boneless pork loin, cut into strips, may be subsituted for the chicken.

Lemon Chicken Herb Stir-Fry

Mandarin Orange Chicken

2 tablespoons rice vinegar
2 tablespoons light soy sauce
2 tablespoons olive oil, divided
2 teaspoons grated orange peel
1 clove garlic, minced
1 pound boneless skinless chicken breasts, cut into strips
2 cans (11 ounces each) mandarin oranges, undrained
½ cup (approximately) orange juice
2 tablespoons cornstarch
½ teaspoon red pepper flakes
1 onion, cut into thin wedges
1 small zucchini, cut into halves and sliced diagonally
1 small yellow squash, cut into halves and sliced diagonally
1 red bell pepper, cut into 1-inch triangles
1 can (3 ounces) chow mein noodles (optional)

180

1. Combine vinegar, soy sauce, 1 tablespoon oil, orange peel and garlic in medium bowl. Add chicken; toss to coat well. Cover and refrigerate 15 minutes to 1 hour.

2. Drain chicken, reserving marinade. Drain oranges, reserving liquid; set oranges aside. Combine marinade from chicken and liquid from oranges in small bowl; add enough orange juice to make 2 cups liquid. Whisk in cornstarch and red pepper flakes; set aside.

3. Heat remaining 1 tablespoon oil in wok or large skillet over high heat. Add chicken; stir-fry 2 to 3 minutes or until no longer pink. Remove chicken; set aside.

4. Stir-fry onion 1 minute over high heat. Add zucchini and squash; stir-fry 1 minute. Add bell pepper; stir-fry 1 minute or until all vegetables are crisp-tender. Add orange juice mixture. Cook and stir until mixture comes to a boil; boil 1 minute. Add chicken, cooking until hot. Add oranges and gently stir. Transfer to serving plate. Top with chow mein noodles, if desired.

Makes 6 servings

Mandarin Orange Chicken

Quick Oriental Feast

1 bag SUCCESS® Brown Rice
Vegetable cooking spray
½ pound skinless, boneless chicken breasts, cut into strips
2 cups sliced fresh mushrooms
1 package (10 ounces) frozen pea pods, thawed and drained
1 can (8 ounces) sliced water chestnuts, drained
6 green onions, chopped
2 teaspoons cornstarch
½ cup reduced-sodium chicken broth
2 teaspoons reduced-sodium soy sauce (optional)

Prepare rice according to package directions.

Spray large skillet with cooking spray. Add chicken; stir-fry over medium-high heat until chicken is no longer pink in center. Remove chicken from skillet; set aside. Spray skillet again with cooking spray. Add mushrooms, pea pods, water chestnuts and onions; stir-fry until tender. Combine cornstarch, chicken broth and soy sauce in small bowl; mix well. Return chicken to skillet. Add cornstarch mixture; cook and stir until sauce is thickened. Serve over hot rice.

Makes 4 servings

Bistro in a Pot

2 teaspoons Lucini Premium Select Extra Virgin Olive Oil
½ to 1 pound boneless skinless chicken, cut into bite-size pieces
½ cup minced shallots
2 large cloves garlic, sliced
2 cups chopped leeks, white and light green parts, washed and drained
1½ cups baby carrots, cut into quarters lengthwise
1 cup thinly sliced new potatoes
3 to 4 teaspoons dried lemon peel
2 tablespoons dried tarragon leaves
1 cup shredded JARLSBERG LITE™ cheese
1 cup frozen peas, thawed (optional)
Minced fresh parsley for garnish

182

In wok or large skillet with cover, heat olive oil over high heat until nearly smoking. Stir-fry chicken, shallots and garlic. Remove to bowl. Add leeks to wok and stir-fry 3 minutes. Add to chicken mixture. Add carrots, potatoes, lemon peel and tarragon to wok; stir-fry 5 minutes. Add chicken mixture to wok. Add ½ cup water; stir quickly. Cover tightly and steam 5 minutes. (Add more water if necessary.)

Remove from heat; add cheese and peas, if desired. Stir and serve.   *Makes 4 to 6 servings*

Serving Suggestion: Serve with a green salad and light sourdough French bread or crusty rolls.

Stir-Fried Pasta with Chicken 'n' Vegetables

    6 ounces angel hair pasta, broken in thirds (about 3 cups)
    ¼ cup *Frank's® RedHot®* Cayenne Pepper Sauce
    3 tablespoons soy sauce
    2 teaspoons cornstarch
    1 tablespoon sugar
    ½ teaspoon garlic powder
    1 pound boneless skinless chicken, cut in ¾-inch cubes
    1 package (16 ounces) frozen stir-fry vegetables

1. Cook pasta in boiling water until just tender. Drain. Combine **Frank's RedHot** Sauce, *¼ cup water,* soy sauce, cornstarch, sugar and garlic powder in small bowl; set aside.

2. Heat *1 tablespoon oil* in large nonstick skillet over high heat. Stir-fry chicken 3 minutes. Add vegetables; stir-fry 3 minutes or until crisp-tender. Add **Frank's RedHot** Sauce mixture. Heat to boiling. Reduce heat to medium-low. Cook, stirring, 1 to 2 minutes or until sauce is thickened.

3. Stir pasta into skillet; toss to coat evenly. Serve hot.   *Makes 4 servings*

Prep Time: 5 minutes
Cook Time: 15 minutes

183

Pad Thai

8 ounces uncooked rice noodles (⅛ inch wide)
2 tablespoons rice wine vinegar
1½ tablespoons fish sauce*
1 to 2 tablespoons fresh lemon juice
1 tablespoon ketchup
2 teaspoons sugar
¼ teaspoon red pepper flakes
1 tablespoon vegetable oil
4 ounces boneless skinless chicken breast, finely chopped
2 green onions, thinly sliced
2 cloves garlic, minced
2 cups fresh bean sprouts
3 ounces small shrimp, peeled
1 medium carrot, shredded
3 tablespoons minced fresh cilantro
2 tablespoons chopped unsalted dry-roasted peanuts

*Fish sauce is available at most larger supermarkets and Asian markets.

1. Place noodles in medium bowl. Cover with lukewarm water; let stand 30 minutes or until soft. Drain and set aside. Whisk rice wine vinegar, fish sauce, lemon juice, ketchup, sugar and red pepper flakes in small bowl; set aside.

2. Heat oil in wok or large nonstick skillet over medium-high heat. Add chicken, green onions and garlic. Cook and stir until chicken is no longer pink. Stir in noodles; cook 1 minute. Add bean sprouts and shrimp; cook just until shrimp turn opaque, about 3 minutes. Stir in fish sauce mixture; toss to coat evenly. Cook until heated through, about 2 minutes.

3. Arrange noodle mixture on platter; sprinkle with carrot, cilantro and peanuts. Garnish with lemon wedges, tomato wedges and additional fresh cilantro, if desired.   *Makes 5 servings*

Pad Thai

Almond Chicken

1½ cups water
4 tablespoons dry sherry, divided
4½ teaspoons plus 1 tablespoon cornstarch, divided
4 teaspoons soy sauce
1 teaspoon instant chicken bouillon granules
1 egg white
½ teaspoon salt
4 whole boneless skinless chicken breasts, cut into 1-inch pieces
  Vegetable oil for frying
½ cup blanched whole almonds (about 3 ounces)
1 large carrot, diced
1 teaspoon minced fresh ginger
6 green onions, cut into 1-inch pieces
3 stalks celery, diagonally cut into ½-inch pieces
8 fresh mushrooms, sliced
½ cup sliced bamboo shoots (½ of 8-ounce can), drained

1. Combine water, 2 tablespoons sherry, 4½ teaspoons cornstarch, soy sauce and bouillon granules in small saucepan. Cook and stir over medium heat until mixture boils and thickens, about 5 minutes. Keep warm.

2. Combine remaining 2 tablespoons sherry, 1 tablespoon cornstarch, egg white and salt in medium bowl. Add chicken pieces; stir to coat well.

3. Heat oil in wok or large skillet over high heat to 375°F. Add half of the chicken pieces, one piece at a time, and cook 3 to 5 minutes until light brown and no longer pink. Drain on paper towels. Repeat with remaining chicken.

4. Remove all but 2 tablespoons oil from wok. Add almonds and stir-fry until golden, about 2 minutes; remove almonds and drain. Add carrot and ginger; stir-fry 1 minute. Add all remaining ingredients; stir-fry until crisp-tender, about 3 minutes. Stir in chicken, almonds and sauce; cook and stir until heated through. *Makes 4 to 6 servings*

Almond Chicken

Shanghai Chicken Fried Rice

4 TYSON® Fresh or Individually Fresh Frozen® Boneless, Skinless Chicken Breasts
2 cups UNCLE BEN'S® Instant Rice
1 tablespoon peanut oil
1 teaspoon grated gingerroot *or* **¼ teaspoon ground ginger**
1 package (16 ounces) frozen vegetables for stir-fry
¼ cup light teriyaki sauce
¼ cup chopped green onions

PREP: CLEAN: Wash hands. Remove protective ice glaze from frozen chicken by holding under cool running water 1 to 2 minutes. Cut chicken into 1-inch pieces. CLEAN: Wash hands.

COOK: Heat oil and gingerroot in large nonstick skillet; add chicken. Cook over medium-high heat until chicken is browned and internal juices run clear. (Or insert instant-read meat thermometer in thickest part of chicken. Temperature should read 170°F.) Stir in vegetables. Cook according to package directions. Meanwhile, prepare rice according to package directions. When vegetables are crisp-tender, stir in rice and teriyaki sauce. Cook until heated through. Sprinkle with green onions.

SERVE: Serve with egg rolls or hot and sour soup, if desired.

CHILL: Refrigerate leftovers immediately.   *Makes 4 servings*

Prep Time: 10 minutes
Cook Time: 20 minutes

Asian Chicken Stir-fry

2 tablespoons cornstarch
1 pound chicken breast tenders, cut into 4 crosswise pieces each
1 tablespoon peanut or canola oil
½ (16-ounce) bag ready-to-cook frozen mixed Asian vegetables
¼ cup teriyaki marinade
½ cup water
   Hot cooked rice

188

1. Place cornstarch and chicken pieces in plastic bag; shake well to coat.

2. Heat oil in 12-inch nonstick skillet over medium-high heat. Add vegetables; stir-fry until tender, 4 to 5 minutes.

3. Push vegetables to one side of pan. Add chicken pieces; stir-fry until no longer pink, about 4 minutes.

4. Add teriyaki marinade and water; bring to boil, stirring constantly, until sauce thickens.

5. Serve immediately over hot cooked rice.   *Makes 6 servings*

Quick Chicken Stir-Fry

4 TYSON® Fresh Boneless, Skinless Chicken Breasts
6 cups cooked UNCLE BEN'S NATURAL SELECT® Chicken & Herb Rice
1 clove garlic, minced
1 package (10 ounces) frozen broccoli, green beans, mushrooms and red peppers
1 medium onion, cut into wedges
⅓ cup shredded carrots
½ cup bottled hoisin sauce

PREP: CLEAN: Wash hands. Cut chicken into ¾-inch pieces. CLEAN: Wash hands.

COOK: Spray large nonstick skillet with nonstick cooking spray. Heat over medium-high heat. Add chicken and garlic; stir-fry 4 minutes. Add frozen vegetables, onion and carrots; stir-fry 3 minutes. Cover; cook 3 to 5 minutes or until vegetables are tender and internal juices of chicken run clear. (Or insert instant-read meat thermometer in thickest part of chicken. Temperature should read 170°F.) Stir in hoisin sauce. Heat thoroughly.

SERVE: Serve chicken and vegetables over hot cooked rice. Garnish with fresh cilantro, if desired.

CHILL: Refrigerate leftovers immediately.   *Makes 6 servings*

Prep Time: 10 minutes
Cook Time: 12 minutes

189

Cashew Chicken

10 ounces boneless skinless chicken breasts, cut into 1×½-inch pieces
1 tablespoon cornstarch
1 tablespoon dry white wine
1 tablespoon reduced-sodium soy sauce
½ teaspoon garlic powder
1 teaspoon vegetable oil
6 green onions, cut into 1-inch pieces
2 cups sliced mushrooms
1 red or green bell pepper, thinly sliced
1 can (6 ounces) sliced water chestnuts, rinsed and drained
2 tablespoons hoisin sauce (optional)
2 cups hot cooked white rice
¼ cup roasted cashews

1. Place chicken in large resealable plastic food storage bag. Blend cornstarch, wine, soy sauce and garlic powder in small bowl until smooth. Pour over chicken pieces. Seal bag; turn to coat. Marinate in refrigerator 1 hour. Drain chicken; discard marinade.

2. Heat oil in wok or large nonstick skillet over medium-high heat until hot. Add onions; stir-fry 1 minute. Add chicken; stir-fry 2 minutes or until browned. Add mushrooms, pepper and water chestnuts; stir-fry 3 minutes or until vegetables are crisp-tender and chicken is no longer pink in center. Stir in hoisin sauce; cook and stir 1 minute or until heated through.

3. Serve chicken and vegetables over rice. Top servings evenly with cashews. Serve immediately. *Makes 4 servings*

 *Helpful Hint*

Hoisin sauce is a traditional Chinese sauce made from soybean paste, garlic, chili peppers, vinegar, sugar and spices. It is sweet and slightly spicy. Store leftover hoisin sauce in a glass jar in the refrigerator—it keeps indefinitely.

190

Cashew Chicken

Santa Fe Spaghetti

8 ounces uncooked thin spaghetti or vermicelli
1 tablespoon vegetable oil
12 ounces boneless chicken or turkey, cut into strips
1½ teaspoons minced garlic
1 teaspoon ground cumin
1 teaspoon ground coriander
¼ teaspoon salt
⅛ teaspoon black pepper
1 package (16 ounces) frozen bell pepper and onion strips for stir-fry, thawed
1½ cups prepared salsa or picante sauce
½ cup sour cream
1½ teaspoons cornstarch
1 tablespoon chopped fresh cilantro or parsley

1. Cook spaghetti according to package directions.

2. Heat oil in large, deep skillet over medium-high heat until hot. Add chicken and garlic. Sprinkle with cumin, coriander, salt and black pepper; stir-fry 2 minutes.

3. Stir in bell peppers and onions and salsa; cook over medium heat 4 minutes. Combine sour cream and cornstarch in small bowl; mix well. Stir into chicken mixture; cook 2 to 3 minutes or until sauce has thickened and chicken is no longer pink in center, stirring occasionally.

4. Drain spaghetti; transfer to four serving plates. Top with chicken mixture; sprinkle with cilantro. *Makes 4 servings*

Prep and Cook Time: 20 minutes

192

Santa Fe Spaghetti

Chicken with Walnuts

1 cup uncooked instant rice
½ cup chicken broth
¼ cup Chinese plum sauce
2 tablespoons soy sauce
2 teaspoons cornstarch
2 tablespoons vegetable oil, divided
3 cups frozen bell peppers and onions
1 pound boneless skinless chicken breasts, cut into ¼-inch slices
1 clove garlic, minced
1 cup walnut halves

1. Cook rice according to package directions.

2. Combine broth, plum sauce, soy sauce and cornstarch; set aside.

3. Heat 1 tablespoon oil in wok or large skillet over medium-high heat until hot. Add frozen peppers and onions; stir-fry 3 minutes or until crisp-tender. Remove vegetables from wok. Drain; discard liquid.

4. Heat remaining 1 tablespoon oil in same wok until hot. Add chicken and garlic; stir-fry 3 minutes or until chicken is no longer pink.

5. Stir broth mixture; add to wok. Cook and stir 1 minute or until sauce thickens. Stir in vegetables and walnuts; cook 1 minute more. Serve with rice.   *Makes 4 servings*

Lighten Up: To reduce sodium, use reduced-sodium chicken broth and reduced-sodium soy sauce. Omit or reduce salt when preparing rice.

Prep and Cook Time: 19 minutes

Plum sauce is a thick Asian sauce made from plums and sometimes apricots, vinegar, chili peppers and spices. Once opened, plum sauce will keep up to one year in a tightly closed glass jar in the refrigerator.

Chicken & Broccoli Stir-Fry with Peanuts

1½ cups fat-free reduced-sodium chicken broth, divided
2 tablespoons reduced-sodium soy sauce
1½ tablespoons cornstarch
½ teaspoon salt
¼ teaspoon ground ginger
¼ teaspoon garlic powder
   Nonstick cooking spray
½ teaspoon vegetable oil
1 pound boneless skinless chicken breasts, cut into 2×¼-inch strips
1 cup small broccoli florets
1 cup red bell pepper strips
¼ cup chopped unsalted dry-roasted peanuts

1. Combine 1 cup chicken broth with soy sauce, cornstarch, salt, ginger and garlic powder in small container. Stir until smooth; set aside.

2. Lightly coat wok with cooking spray; heat over high heat until hot. Add oil; tilt wok to coat bottom. Add chicken; stir-fry 2 minutes or until no longer pink. Remove chicken from wok.

3. Add remaining ½ cup chicken broth to wok; bring to a boil. Add broccoli and bell pepper; return to a boil. Reduce heat and simmer, covered, 2 minutes or until broccoli is crisp-tender.

4. Increase heat to high. Add chicken. Stir cornstarch mixture and add to wok. Bring to a boil; boil 1 to 2 minutes or until thickened. Stir in peanuts.   *Makes 4 servings (1 cup each)*

195

You can reduce fat by using less oil in stir-fries. This recipe uses the technique of lightly coating the wok with cooking spray, heating it, then adding oil. The coating of cooking spray allows the small amount of oil to cling to the surface of the wok.

Quick 'n' Tangy Beef Stir-Fry

SAUCE
- ½ cup *French's*® **Worcestershire Sauce**
- ½ cup water
- 2 tablespoons sugar
- 2 teaspoons cornstarch
- ½ teaspoon ground ginger
- ½ teaspoon garlic powder

STIR-FRY
- 1 pound thinly sliced beef steak
- 3 cups sliced bell peppers

1. Combine ingredients for sauce. Marinate beef in ¼ *cup* sauce 5 minutes. Heat *1 tablespoon oil* in large skillet or wok over high heat. Stir-fry beef in batches 5 minutes or until browned.

2. Add peppers; cook 2 minutes. Add remaining sauce; stir-fry until sauce thickens. Serve over hot cooked rice or ramen noodles, if desired.   *Makes 4 servings*

196

Prep Time: 10 minutes
Cook Time: about 10 minutes

Sir-frying is a quick-cooking method in which pieces of meat and vegetables are cooked over high heat. To ensure even cooking and prevent burning, meat and vegetables should be stirred constantly. It is important to prepare all ingredients before beginning to cook.

Quick 'n' Tangy Beef Stir-Fry

Five-Spice Beef Stir-Fry

1 pound beef top sirloin, cut into thin strips
2 tablespoons reduced-sodium soy sauce
2 tablespoons plus 1½ teaspoons cornstarch, divided
3 tablespoons walnut or vegetable oil, divided
4 medium carrots, cut into matchstick-size pieces (about 2 cups)
1 red bell pepper, cut into chunks
1 yellow bell pepper, cut into chunks
1 cup chopped onion
¼ to ½ teaspoon red pepper flakes
1 tablespoon plus 1½ teaspoons packed dark brown sugar
2 teaspoons beef bouillon granules
1 teaspoon Chinese five-spice powder
3 cups hot cooked rice
½ cup honey-roasted peanuts

1. Place beef in shallow glass baking dish. Combine soy sauce and 2 tablespoons cornstarch in small bowl. Pour soy sauce mixture over beef; toss to coat thoroughly. Set aside.

2. Meanwhile, add 1 tablespoon oil to large nonstick skillet or wok. Heat skillet over high heat 1 minute or until hot. Add carrots. Stir-fry 3 to 4 minutes or until edges begin to brown. Remove carrots and set aside.

3. Reduce heat to medium-high. Add 1 tablespoon oil, bell peppers, onion and red pepper flakes; stir-fry 4 minutes or until onions are translucent. Remove vegetables and set aside separately from carrots.

4. Add remaining 1 tablespoon oil to skillet. Add beef; stir-fry 6 minutes.

5. Meanwhile, in small bowl, combine 1½ cups water with brown sugar, bouillon granules, five-spice powder and remaining 1½ teaspoons cornstarch. Stir until smooth.

6. Increase heat to high. Add bouillon mixture and reserved bell peppers and onions; bring to a boil. Cook and stir 2 to 3 minutes or until slightly thickened.

7. Toss rice with carrots; place on serving platter. Spoon beef mixture over rice and sprinkle peanuts over beef mixture. *Makes 4 servings*

Five-Spice Beef Stir-Fry

Honey Dijon Beef and Vegetable Stir-Fry

⅔ cup HEINZ® Tomato Ketchup
2 tablespoons honey Dijon mustard
1 tablespoon soy sauce
1 pound boneless beef sirloin steak, cut into thin strips
1 red bell pepper, cut into thin strips
1 onion, cut into thin wedges
2 cups broccoli florets
  Hot cooked rice

In small bowl, combine ketchup, ⅓ cup water, mustard and soy sauce; set aside. In large preheated nonstick skillet, quickly brown beef; remove. Cook pepper, onion and broccoli, stirring, until crisp-tender, about 4 minutes. Return beef to skillet and stir in reserved ketchup mixture; heat. Serve with rice. *Makes 4 servings*

Cantonese Sweet & Sour Pork

1 egg, well beaten
1 tablespoon cornstarch
1 tablespoon all-purpose flour
1 pound lean boneless pork, cut into 1-inch pieces
3 cups WESSON® Oil
1 teaspoon minced fresh garlic
1 teaspoon minced fresh gingerroot
1 green bell pepper, cut into 1-inch pieces
1 onion, cut into chunks
1 can (8 ounces) LA CHOY® Bamboo Shoots, drained
1 can (8 ounces) LA CHOY® Sliced Water Chestnuts, drained
2 jars (10 ounces each) LA CHOY® Sweet & Sour Sauce
2 teaspoons LA CHOY® Soy Sauce
  Hot cooked rice
1 can (5 ounces) LA CHOY® Chow Mein Noodles

In medium bowl, combine egg, cornstarch and flour. Add pork; toss gently. In large saucepan, heat oil to 350°F. Carefully add pork a few pieces at a time; deep-fry 3 minutes. Remove pork from oil; drain on paper towels. Let stand 5 minutes. Meanwhile, repeat with remaining pieces of pork. Return pork to hot oil; continue deep frying until golden brown. Remove pork from oil; drain again. Remove all but 2 tablespoons oil from saucepan. Add garlic and ginger to saucepan; cook and stir 30 seconds. Add green pepper and onion; stir-fry 2 minutes or until crisp-tender. Stir in all remaining ingredients except rice and noodles; bring to a boil. Return pork to saucepan; heat thoroughly, stirring occasionally. Serve over rice. Sprinkle with noodles.

Makes 4 to 6 servings

Broccoli Beef Stir-Fry

½ cup beef broth
4 tablespoons HOLLAND HOUSE® Sherry Cooking Wine, divided
2 tablespoons soy sauce
1 tablespoon cornstarch
1 teaspoon sugar
2 tablespoons vegetable oil, divided
2 cups fresh broccoli florets
1 cup fresh snow peas
1 red bell pepper, cut into strips
1 pound boneless top round or sirloin steak, slightly frozen, cut into thin strips
1 clove garlic, minced
4 cups hot cooked rice

1. To make sauce, in small bowl, combine broth, 2 tablespoons of cooking wine, soy sauce, cornstarch and sugar. Mix well and set aside. In large skillet or wok, heat 1 tablespoon oil. Stir-fry broccoli, snow peas and bell pepper 1 minute. Add remaining 2 tablespoons cooking wine.

2. Cover; cook 1 to 2 minutes. Remove from pan. Heat remaining 1 tablespoon oil; add meat and garlic. Stir-fry 5 minutes or until meat is browned. Add sauce to meat; cook 2 to 3 minutes or until thickened, stirring frequently. Add vegetables and heat through. Serve over cooked rice.

Makes 4 servings

201

Shredded Orange Beef

2 tablespoons soy sauce, divided
3 teaspoons cornstarch, divided
1½ teaspoons Asian sesame oil
1 egg white
1 small beef flank steak (about 1 pound), cut into strips
1 tablespoon sugar
1 tablespoon dry sherry
1 tablespoon white vinegar
2 cups vegetable oil
4 medium carrots, cut into julienne strips
2 tablespoons orange peel slivers
4 green onions with tops, cut into slivers
2 to 3 fresh red or green jalapeño peppers,* cut into strips
2 cloves garlic, minced

*Jalapeño peppers can sting and irritate the skin; wear rubber gloves when handling peppers and do not touch eyes. Wash hands after handling peppers.

1. Whisk together 1 tablespoon soy sauce, 1 teaspoon cornstarch, sesame oil and egg white in medium bowl. Add beef; toss to coat. Let beef marinate while preparing vegetables. Combine sugar, sherry, vinegar, remaining 1 tablespoon soy sauce and 2 teaspoons cornstarch in small bowl; mix well. Set aside.

2. Heat vegetable oil in wok over medium-high heat until oil registers 375°F on deep-fry thermometer. Add carrots and fry about 3 minutes or until tender. Remove carrots with slotted spoon and place in large strainer set over medium bowl. Reheat oil and fry orange peel about 15 seconds or until fragrant. Remove to paper towels; drain.

3. To double-fry beef,** add beef to wok; fry 1 minute or just until meat turns light in color. Remove beef to strainer placed over large bowl. Reheat oil to 375°F. Place ⅓ of drained beef in oil and fry about 3 minutes or until browned. Transfer beef to strainer with carrots. Repeat with remaining beef in two batches, reheating oil to maintain temperature.

4. Pour off all oil from wok. Reheat wok over medium-high heat. Add onions, chilies and garlic; stir-fry 30 seconds. Stir cornstarch mixture and add to wok. Cook and stir until sauce thickens. Add beef, carrots and orange peel; stir-fry until hot.   *Makes 4 servings*

**This technique helps keep the meat moist inside and crispy on the outside. The first frying "seals" in the juices while the second frying cooks the meat until crisp.

Shredded Orange Beef

Orange Beef and Broccoli

1 pound lean boneless beef, cut 1 inch thick
½ cup orange juice
2 teaspoons reduced-sodium soy sauce
1 teaspoon sugar
3 teaspoons vegetable oil, divided
¾ pound broccoli, coarsely chopped
1 cup diagonally sliced carrots
½ cup thinly sliced red bell pepper
1 green onion, diagonally sliced
¾ cup cold water
2 teaspoons cornstarch
1 tablespoon grated orange peel
6 ounces uncooked yolk-free wide noodles

1. Slice beef across grain into ⅛-inch slices; place beef in nonmetallic bowl. Add orange juice, soy sauce and sugar; toss to coat evenly. Let stand 30 minutes, or cover and refrigerate overnight.

2. Heat 2 teaspoons oil in large nonstick skillet or wok over medium-high heat until hot. Add broccoli, carrots, bell pepper and green onion; cook and stir 2 minutes. Remove vegetables to large bowl.

3. Drain beef; reserve marinade. Heat remaining 1 teaspoon oil in same skillet over medium-high heat until hot. Add beef to skillet; cook 1 to 2 minutes or until no longer pink. Add vegetables and reserved marinade to skillet; bring to a boil. Stir water into cornstarch until smooth; add to skillet. Cook until thickened, stirring constantly. Sprinkle with grated orange peel.

4. Cook noodles according to package directions, omitting salt; drain. Spoon beef mixture over noodles; serve immediately. *Makes 4 servings*

Orange Beef and Broccoli

Stir-Fried Beef and Vegetables

⅔ cup beef broth or stock

2 tablespoons soy sauce

   Pinch of ground cinnamon

¼ teaspoon freshly ground black pepper

2 teaspoons cornstarch

2 tablespoons cold water

3 tablespoons CRISCO® Oil*

1 tablespoon chopped fresh ginger

2 teaspoons minced garlic *or* 1 large garlic clove, peeled and minced

1 pound lean beef, such as flank steak or boneless sirloin, trimmed and cut into
   ¼-inch-thick slices

1 carrot, peeled and thinly sliced

1 bunch scallions (or green onions), trimmed and cut into 1-inch pieces

¼ pound fresh snow peas, rinsed and stems removed

*Use your favorite Crisco Oil product.

1. Combine broth, soy sauce, cinnamon and pepper in small bowl. Set aside. Combine cornstarch and water in small bowl. Stir to dissolve.

2. Heat oil in wok or large skillet on medium-high heat. Add ginger and garlic. Stir-fry 30 seconds. Add beef, carrot and scallions. Stir-fry 3 minutes, or until beef is no longer red. Add broth mixture. Cook 2 minutes. Add snow peas. Cook 2 minutes, or until snow peas are bright green. Stir in cornstarch mixture. Cook 1 minute, or until thickened. Serve immediately.

Makes 4 servings

Note: Other vegetables can be used in place of those specified. Broccoli flowerets or sliced celery can be used in place of the carrot. Cooking time will be the same. In place of scallions, 1 medium onion, peeled and sliced, can be substituted. Fresh or frozen green peas can be used in place of snow peas.

Tip: If using canned broth, pour the remainder of the can into an ice cube tray and freeze. Once frozen, store the cubes in an air-tight plastic bag. That way you'll always have the few tablespoons of stock needed for many recipes.

Tip: It's easier to slice meat thinly if it's partially frozen. Wrap the steak in plastic wrap and freeze for 15 minutes. Always cut meat against the grain unless a recipe specifically says to slice it with the grain.

Preparation Time: 25 minutes
Total Time: 35 minutes

Vegetable Pork Stir-Fry

¾ **pound pork tenderloin**
1 **tablespoon vegetable oil**
1½ **cups (about 6 ounces) sliced fresh mushrooms**
1 **large green pepper, cut into strips**
1 **zucchini, thinly sliced**
2 **ribs celery, cut into diagonal slices**
1 **cup thinly sliced carrots**
1 **clove garlic, minced**
1 **cup chicken broth**
2 **tablespoons reduced-sodium soy sauce**
1½ **tablespoons cornstarch**
3 **cups hot cooked rice**

Slice pork across the grain into ⅛-inch strips. Brown pork strips in oil in large skillet over medium-high heat. Push meat to side of skillet. Add mushrooms, pepper, zucchini, celery, carrots and garlic; stir-fry about 3 minutes. Combine broth, soy sauce and cornstarch. Add to skillet and cook, stirring, until thickened; cook 1 minute longer. Serve over rice.

Makes 6 servings

*Favorite recipe from **USA Rice Federation***

 *Vegetables for stir-fries are sometimes cut on a diagonal. This increases the surface area that is in contact with the hot oil and shortens cooking time. Diagonal cuts also look attractive.*

Cantonese Tomato Beef

2 tablespoons soy sauce

2 tablespoons Asian sesame oil, divided

1 tablespoon plus 1 teaspoon cornstarch, divided

1 small beef flank steak or filet mignon tail (about 1 pound), trimmed and
   cut into 2×¼-inch strips

1 pound fresh Chinese-style thin wheat noodles *or* 12 ounces uncooked spaghetti

1 cup beef broth

2 tablespoons brown sugar

1 tablespoon cider vinegar

2 tablespoons vegetable oil, divided

1 tablespoon minced fresh ginger

3 small onions (about 7 ounces), cut into wedges

2 pounds ripe tomatoes (5 large), cored and cut into wedges

1 green onion with tops, diagonally cut into thin slices
   Edible flowers, such as nasturtium, for garnish

1. Combine soy sauce, 1 tablespoon sesame oil and 1 teaspoon cornstarch in large bowl. Add beef strips; toss to coat. Set aside to marinate.

2. Cook noodles according to package directions just until tender. Combine beef broth, sugar, remaining 1 tablespoon cornstarch and vinegar in small bowl; mix until smooth. Set aside.

3. Drain cooked noodles in colander and return to stockpot. Add remaining 1 tablespoon sesame oil; toss. Keep warm.

4. Heat wok over high heat 1 minute or until hot. Drizzle 1 tablespoon vegetable oil into wok and heat 30 seconds. Add ginger and stir-fry about 30 seconds or until fragrant. Add beef mixture and stir-fry 5 minutes or until lightly browned. Remove beef to bowl and set aside. Reduce heat to medium.

5. Add remaining 1 tablespoon vegetable oil to wok. Add onion wedges; cook and stir about 2 minutes or until wilted. Stir in ½ of tomato wedges. Stir broth mixture and add to wok. Cook and stir until liquid boils and thickens.

6. Return beef and any juices to wok. Add remaining tomato wedges; cook and stir until heated through. Place cooked noodles in shallow serving bowl. Spoon tomato beef mixture over noodles. Sprinkle with green onion. Garnish, if desired.   *Makes 4 servings*

Cantonese Tomato Beef

Green Dragon Stir-Fry

2 tablespoons vegetable oil, divided
1 pound beef flank steak, very thinly sliced
1 bunch asparagus *or* 8 ounces green beans, cut into 2-inch pieces
1 green bell pepper, cut into strips
1 cup julienne carrots
3 large green onions, sliced
1 tablespoon minced fresh ginger
1 clove garlic, minced
¼ cup water
1 tablespoon soy sauce
1 tablespoon TABASCO® brand Green Pepper Sauce
½ teaspoon salt
2 cups hot cooked rice (optional)

Heat 1 tablespoon oil in 12-inch skillet over medium-high heat. Add flank steak; cook until well browned on all sides, stirring frequently. Remove steak to plate with slotted spoon.

Heat remaining 1 tablespoon oil in skillet over medium heat. Add asparagus, green bell pepper, carrots, green onions, ginger and garlic; cook about 3 minutes, stirring frequently. Add water, soy sauce, TABASCO® Green Pepper Sauce, salt and steak; heat to boiling over high heat.

Reduce heat to low; simmer, uncovered, 3 minutes, stirring occasionally. Serve with rice, if desired. *Makes 4 servings*

Note: Stir-fry is also delicious served over ramen or soba noodles.

Green Dragon Stir-Fry

Jambalaya Stir-Fry on Cajun Rice

1¾ cups water
1 cup uncooked converted rice
1 can (16 ounces) diced tomatoes, undrained
½ cup finely chopped celery
2 teaspoons chicken bouillon granules
1 bay leaf
8 ounces andouille sausage, cut into ¼-inch rounds*
1½ cups chopped onions
1 cup chopped green bell pepper
½ pound raw large shrimp, peeled and deveined
½ pound boneless chicken breasts, cut into 1-inch pieces
¾ teaspoon dried thyme leaves
¼ cup chopped fresh parsley
1 teaspoon salt
½ teaspoon ground red pepper
½ teaspoon paprika
Hot pepper sauce

*If andouille sausage is not available, use kielbasa sausage.

1. Bring water to a boil in medium saucepan. Add rice, tomatoes with juice, celery, bouillon granules and bay leaf. Return to a boil; reduce heat, cover tightly and simmer 20 minutes or until all liquid is absorbed. Remove and discard bay leaf.

2. Meanwhile, heat large skillet over medium-high heat 1 minute. Add sausage, onions and bell pepper; cook and stir 10 minutes.

3. Increase heat to high; add shrimp, chicken and thyme. Cook and stir 5 minutes. Add parsley, salt, ground red pepper and paprika. Stir to blend thoroughly.

4. Place rice on platter. Spoon shrimp mixture over rice and serve with pepper sauce.

Makes 4 servings

Ginger Beef & Noodle Stir-Fry

1 pound flank steak, cut into thin strips
½ cup LAWRY'S® Thai Ginger Marinade with Lime Juice
1 tablespoon vegetable oil
2 cups broccoli florettes
1 red bell pepper, chopped
2 tablespoons soy sauce
1 teaspoon cornstarch
1 teaspoon LAWRY'S® Garlic Powder with Parsley
1 package (7 ounces) chuka soba noodles (Japanese-style noodles) prepared according to package directions

In large resealable plastic food storage bag, combine beef and Thai Ginger Marinade with Lime Juice; seal bag. Marinate in refrigerator at least 30 minutes. In large skillet, heat oil. Add broccoli and bell pepper. Stir-Fry over high heat 2 minutes; remove and set aside. Remove steak; discard used marinade. In same skillet cook beef over high heat about 5 to 7 minutes. In small bowl combine soy sauce, cornstarch and Garlic Powder with Parsley; mix well. Add to beef; cook over medium heat until sauce is thickened. Stir in broccoli and bell pepper; heat through. Spoon over noodles.

Makes 4 servings

Serving Suggestion: Serve with flat rice crackers.

Hint: Vermicelli noodles may be substituted for chuka soba noodles.

Marinating adds flavor to meat. If the marinade contains an acidic ingredient, such as citrus juice or vinegar, it will also tenderize meat. It is best to marinate meat in the refrigerator rather than at room temperature.

Five-Spice Shrimp with Walnuts

    1 pound medium or large raw shrimp, peeled and deveined
    ½ teaspoon Chinese five-spice powder
    2 cloves garlic, minced
    ½ cup chicken broth
    2 tablespoons soy sauce
    2 tablespoons dry sherry
    1 tablespoon cornstarch
    1 tablespoon peanut or vegetable oil
    1 large red bell pepper, cut into short, thin strips
    ⅓ cup walnut halves or quarters
       Hot cooked white rice (optional)
    ¼ cup thinly sliced green onions (optional)

1. Toss shrimp with five-spice powder and garlic in small bowl.

2. Blend broth, soy sauce and sherry into cornstarch in cup until smooth.

3. Heat wok or large skillet over medium-high heat. Add oil; heat until hot. Add shrimp mixture, bell pepper and walnuts; stir-fry 3 to 5 minutes until shrimp are opaque and bell pepper is crisp-tender.

4. Stir broth mixture and add to wok. Stir-fry 1 minute or until sauce boils and thickens. Serve over rice, if desired. Garnish with onions. *Makes 4 servings*

215

Five spice powder is a mixture of ground cinnamon, cloves, star anise, fennel, Szechuan peppercorns and sometimes additional ingredients. It is used to flavor some Chinese dishes. It is available in Asian markets and large supermarkets.

Garlic Shrimp & Vegetables

2 tablespoons butter
1 tablespoon olive oil
1 bunch green onions, chopped
1 red bell pepper, diced
1 pound peeled, deveined large shrimp
2 cloves garlic, minced
   Juice of 1 lime
   Salt and pepper, to taste
   Hot cooked spinach fetuccine (optional)

1. Heat butter and oil in wok over medium heat. Add onions and red pepper. Stir-fry 2 minutes or until vegetables are crisp-tender.

2. Add shrimp and garlic; stir-fry 2 minutes or until shrimp turn pink.

3. Stir in lime juice. Season with salt and black pepper. Serve over fettuccine, if desired.

Makes 4 servings

216

The wok is commonly associated with the Asian technique of stir-frying, but it can also be used to braise, deep fry, simmer, smoke and steam. When buying a wok for stir-frying, choose a 14-inch range top wok or an electric model.

Chicken Tortilla Soup

1 clove garlic, minced
1 can (14½ ounces) chicken broth
1 jar (16 ounces) mild chunky-style salsa
2 tablespoons *Frank's® RedHot®* Cayenne Pepper Sauce
1 package (10 ounces) fully cooked carved chicken breasts
1 can (8¾ ounces) whole kernel corn, undrained
1 tablespoon chopped fresh cilantro (optional)
1 cup crushed tortilla chips
½ cup (2 ounces) shredded Monterey Jack cheese

1. Heat *1 teaspoon oil* in large saucepan over medium-high heat. Cook garlic 1 minute or until tender. Add broth, *¾ cup water,* salsa and **Frank's RedHot** Sauce. Stir in chicken, corn and cilantro. Heat to boiling. Reduce heat to medium-low. Cook, covered, 5 minutes.

2. Stir in tortillas and cheese. Serve hot. *Makes 4 servings*

Prep Time: 5 minutes
Cook Time: 6 minutes

Shrug off the chill of

a cold blustery day

with a steaming bowl

of delicious

homemade soup. Add

bread or a salad and

you have a simple

but filling meal.

Chicken Tortilla Soup

Cream of Chicken and Wild Rice Soup

½ cup uncooked wild rice
5 cups canned chicken broth, divided
¼ cup butter
1 large carrot, sliced
1 medium onion, chopped
2 ribs celery, chopped
¼ pound fresh mushrooms, sliced
2 tablespoons all-purpose flour
¼ teaspoon salt
¼ teaspoon white pepper
1½ cups chopped cooked chicken
¼ cup dry sherry

1. Rinse rice thoroughly in fine strainer under cold running water; drain.

2. Combine 2½ cups chicken broth and rice in 2-quart saucepan. Bring to a boil over medium-high heat. Reduce heat to low; simmer, covered, 45 to 50 minutes or until rice is tender. Drain; set aside.

3. Melt butter in 3-quart saucepan over medium heat. Add carrot; cook and stir 3 minutes. Add onion, celery and mushrooms; cook and stir 3 to 4 minutes until vegetables are tender. Remove from heat. Whisk in flour, salt and pepper until smooth.

4. Gradually stir in remaining 2½ cups chicken broth. Bring to a boil over medium heat; cook and stir 1 minute or until thickened. Stir in chicken and sherry. Reduce heat to low; simmer, uncovered, 3 minutes or until heated through.

5. Spoon ¼ cup cooked rice into each serving bowl. Ladle soup over rice.

Makes 4 to 6 servings

220

Cream of Chicken and Wild Rice Soup

Mexicali Chicken Soup

1 package (1¼ ounces) taco seasoning, divided
12 ounces boneless skinless chicken thighs
   Nonstick cooking spray
2 cans (14½ ounces each) stewed tomatoes with onions, celery and green peppers
1 package (9 ounces) frozen green beans
1 package (10 ounces) frozen corn
1 cup chicken broth
4 cups tortilla chips

1. Place half of taco seasoning in small bowl. Cut chicken thighs into 1-inch pieces; coat with taco seasoning.

2. Coat large nonstick skillet with nonstick cooking spray. Cook and stir chicken 5 minutes over medium heat. Add tomatoes, beans, corn, broth and remaining taco seasoning; bring to a boil. Reduce heat to medium-low; simmer 10 minutes. Top with tortilla chips before serving.

Makes 4 servings

Serving Suggestion: Serve nachos with the soup. Spread tortilla chips on a plate; dot with salsa and sprinkle with cheese. Heat just until the cheese is melted.

Salsa Corn Soup with Chicken

3 quarts chicken broth
2 pounds boneless skinless chicken breasts, cooked and diced
2 packages (10 ounces each) frozen whole kernel corn, thawed
4 jars (11 ounces each) NEWMAN'S OWN® All Natural Salsa
4 large carrots, diced

Bring chicken broth to a boil in Dutch oven. Add chicken, corn, Newman's Own® Salsa and carrots. Bring to a boil. Reduce heat and simmer until carrots are tender.   *Makes 8 servings*

Mexicali Chicken Soup

Turkey Chowder

2 tablespoons butter or margarine
½ cup chopped carrot
½ cup chopped celery
½ cup chopped onion
⅓ cup uncooked rice
⅓ cup barley
2 cans (14½ ounces each) chicken broth
½ teaspoon dried thyme leaves
2 cups chopped cooked turkey
1 package (10 ounces) frozen corn, thawed
½ cup half-and-half
   Salt and pepper

1. Melt butter in large saucepan. Add carrot, celery and onion; cook and stir until tender. Stir in rice and barley; cook 2 minutes. Add broth and thyme; bring to a boil. Reduce heat to low; simmer 20 to 25 minutes or until rice and barley are tender. Add turkey and corn; cook 5 minutes or until heated through. Add half-and-half; heat, but do not boil. Season with salt and pepper to taste.

2. Ladle chowder into bowls. Garnish, if desired. *Makes 5 servings*

Chicken Tortellini Soup

1 can (49½ ounces) chicken broth
1 package PERDUE® SHORT CUTS® Fresh Italian Carved Chicken Breast
1 package (9 ounces) fresh pesto or cheese tortellini or tortelloni
1 cup fresh spinach or arugula leaves, shredded
¼ to ½ cup grated Parmesan cheese

In large saucepan over medium-high heat, bring broth to a boil. Add chicken and tortellini; cook 6 to 8 minutes, until pasta is tender, reducing heat to keep a gentle boil. Just before serving, stir in fresh spinach. Ladle soup into bowls and sprinkle with Parmesan cheese.

Makes 4 servings

Prep Time: 5 minutes
Cook Time: 15 minutes

Louisiana Shrimp and Chicken Gumbo

3 tablespoons vegetable oil
¼ cup flour
2 medium onions, chopped
1 cup chopped celery
1 large green bell pepper, chopped
2 cloves garlic, minced
3 cups chicken broth
1 (16-ounce) can whole tomatoes in juice, undrained
1 (10-ounce) package frozen sliced okra
1 bay leaf
1 teaspoon TABASCO® brand Pepper Sauce
¾ pound shredded cooked chicken
½ pound raw shrimp, peeled, deveined
Hot cooked rice

Heat oil in large saucepan or Dutch oven. Add flour and cook over low heat until mixture turns dark brown and develops a nutty aroma, stirring frequently. Add onions, celery, bell pepper and garlic; cook 5 minutes or until vegetables are tender. Gradually add broth. Stir in tomatoes with juice, okra, bay leaf and TABASCO® Sauce; bring to a boil. Add chicken and shrimp; cook 3 to 5 minutes or until shrimp turn pink. Remove bay leaf. Serve with rice.

Makes 6 servings

225

Okra is native to northern Africa; it is often used in Creole cooking. When cooked, okra develops a gumminess that makes it a good thickener for soups and stews, especially gumbos.

Chicken-Barley Soup

1½ **pounds chicken thighs, skinned**
2 **medium ribs celery, sliced**
2 **medium carrots, peeled and thinly sliced**
1 **small leek, sliced**
6 **cups cold water**
1½ **teaspoons salt**
½ **teaspoon dried marjoram leaves**
¼ **teaspoon black pepper**
¼ **teaspoon dried summer savory leaves**
1 **herb bouquet**
⅓ **cup quick-cooking barley**
3 **cups fresh spinach (loosely packed), chopped**
¼ **small red bell pepper, cut into matchsticks**
Salt and black pepper to taste
Celery leaves for garnish

Place chicken, celery, carrots, leek, water, salt, marjoram, black pepper, savory and herb bouquet in 5-quart Dutch oven. Bring to a boil. Reduce heat; simmer, uncovered, 45 minutes or until chicken is tender.

Remove chicken from soup and let cool slightly. Remove herb bouquet; discard. Skim foam and fat from soup using large spoon.

Add barley to soup. Bring to a boil. Reduce heat; simmer, uncovered, 10 minutes or until barley is almost tender. Meanwhile, remove chicken meat from bones; discard bones. Cut chicken into bite-size pieces. Stir chicken, spinach and bell pepper into soup. Simmer 5 minutes or until spinach is wilted, chicken is heated and bell pepper is tender. Season with additional salt and black pepper.   *Makes 6 servings*

Helpful Hint

Use any combination of herbs and spices, such as parsley stems, thyme sprigs, peppercorns, whole cloves, bay leaves and garlic cloves for an herb bouquet. Wrap in squares of cheesecloth and tie bundles with kitchen string.

Chicken-Barley Soup

Ravioli Soup

1 package (9 ounces) fresh or frozen cheese ravioli or tortellini
¾ pound hot Italian sausage, crumbled
1 can (14½ ounces) DEL MONTE® Stewed Tomatoes Italian Recipe
1 can (14½ ounces) beef broth
1 can (14½ ounces) DEL MONTE® Italian Beans, drained
2 green onions, sliced

1. Cook pasta according to package directions; drain.

2. Meanwhile, cook sausage in 5-quart pot over medium-high heat until no longer pink; drain. Add undrained tomatoes, broth and 1¾ cups water; bring to boil.

3. Reduce heat to low; stir in pasta, green beans and green onions. Simmer until heated through. Season with pepper and sprinkle with grated Parmesan cheese, if desired.

Makes 4 servings

Prep and Cook Time: 15 minutes

228

Quick & Easy Meatball Soup

1 package (15 to 18 ounces) frozen Italian sausage meatballs without sauce
2 cans (about 14 ounces each) Italian-style stewed tomatoes
2 cans (about 14 ounces each) beef broth
1 can (about 14 ounces) mixed vegetables
½ cup uncooked rotini or small macaroni
½ teaspoon dried oregano leaves

1. Thaw meatballs in microwave oven according to package directions.

2. Place remaining ingredients in large saucepan. Add meatballs. Bring to boil. Reduce heat; cover and simmer 15 minutes or until pasta is tender.

Makes 4 to 6 servings

Ravioli Soup

Zesty Noodle Soup

1 pound BOB EVANS® Zesty Hot Roll Sausage
1 (16-ounce) can whole tomatoes, undrained
½ pound fresh mushrooms, sliced
1 large onion, chopped
1 small green bell pepper, chopped
2½ cups tomato juice
2½ cups water
¼ cup chopped fresh parsley
1 teaspoon lemon juice
1 teaspoon Worcestershire sauce
1 teaspoon celery seeds
½ teaspoon salt
½ teaspoon dried thyme leaves
1 cup uncooked egg noodles

230

Crumble sausage into 3-quart saucepan. Cook over medium-high heat until browned, stirring occasionally. Drain off any drippings. Add tomatoes with juice, mushrooms, onion and pepper; cook until vegetables are tender, stirring well to break up tomatoes. Stir in all remaining ingredients except noodles. Bring to a boil over high heat. Reduce heat to low; simmer, covered, 30 minutes. Add noodles; simmer just until noodles are tender, yet firm. Serve hot. Refrigerate leftovers. *Makes 6 servings*

Serving Suggestion: Serve with crusty French bread.

Veg•All® Black Bean Soup

1 package (14 ounces) smoked sausage, cut into ½-inch slices
2 cans (15 ounces each) VEG•ALL® Original Mixed Vegetables
2 cans (15 ounces each) black beans with spices
1 can (14½ ounces) chicken broth

In large soup kettle, lightly brown sausage. Add Veg•All, beans and chicken broth; heat until hot. Serve immediately. *Makes 4 to 6 servings*

Zesty Noodle Soup

Cheesy Potato Soup

4 baking potatoes (about 1½ pounds)
1 medium onion, sliced
2 tablespoons butter
2 tablespoons all-purpose flour
1 teaspoon beef bouillon granules
1 can (12 ounces) evaporated milk
4 ounces Wisconsin Brick cheese, cut into 1-inch cubes
1 teaspoon chopped fresh parsley
¾ teaspoon salt
¾ teaspoon black pepper
¾ teaspoon Worcestershire sauce

MICROWAVE DIRECTIONS

Microwave potatoes at HIGH until tender; cool. Place onion and butter in large microwavable bowl. Cook at HIGH until tender, about 2 minutes. Stir in flour. Add bouillon and 2 cups water; stir well. Cook at HIGH 2 minutes or until hot. Scoop out potatoes, leaving pieces in chunks; discard skins. Add potatoes, milk, cheese and seasonings to onion mixture. Microwave at HIGH 2½ to 4 minutes or until cheese is melted and soup is hot. *Makes 6 servings*

*Favorite recipe from **Wisconsin Milk Marketing Board***

Brazilian Black Bean Soup

1 red onion, chopped
2 cloves garlic, minced
1 can (29 ounces) black beans, drained
1 can (14½ ounces) vegetable or chicken broth
3 tablespoons *Frank's® RedHot®* Cayenne Pepper Sauce
2 tablespoons chopped cilantro
2 teaspoons ground cumin
2 tablespoons rum or sherry (optional)

1. Heat *1 tablespoon oil* in 3-quart saucepot. Cook and stir onion and garlic 3 minutes or just until tender. Stir in *1½ cups water* and remaining ingredients *except* rum. Heat to boiling.

Reduce heat to medium-low. Cook, partially covered, 20 minutes or until flavors are blended, stirring occasionally.

2. Ladle about half of soup into blender or food processor. Cover securely. Process on low speed until mixture is smooth. Return to saucepot. Stir in rum. Cook over medium-low heat 3 minutes or until heated through and flavors are blended. Garnish with lime slices, sour cream, minced onion or cilantro, if desired. *Makes 4 to 6 servings*

Prep Time: 10 minutes
Cook Time: 30 minutes

SPAM™ Western Bean Soup

1 cup chopped onion
1 tablespoon vegetable oil
3 (10½-ounce) cans condensed chicken broth
1 (14½-ounce) can tomatoes, cut up
1 cup sliced carrots
⅓ cup chili sauce
3 tablespoons packed brown sugar
3 tablespoons cider vinegar
2 teaspoons Worcestershire sauce
2 teaspoons prepared mustard
2 (15½-ounce) cans pinto beans, rinsed and drained
1 (12-ounce) can SPAM® Classic, cubed
2 tablespoons chopped fresh parsley

In 5-quart saucepan, sauté onion in oil until golden. Stir in chicken broth, tomatoes, carrots, chili sauce, brown sugar, vinegar, Worcestershire sauce and mustard. Mash half the beans with fork; add mashed beans and whole beans to soup. Blend well. Bring to a boil. Cover. Reduce heat and simmer 30 minutes or until carrots are tender. Stir in SPAM® and parsley. Simmer 2 minutes. *Makes 6 servings*

233

Split Pea Soup

1 package (16 ounces) dried green or yellow split peas
1 pound smoked pork hocks *or* 4 ounces smoked sausage links, sliced and quartered *or*
   1 meaty ham bone
7 cups water
1 medium onion, chopped
2 medium carrots, chopped
¾ teaspoon salt
½ teaspoon dried basil leaves
¼ teaspoon dried oregano leaves
¼ teaspoon black pepper
   Ham and carrot strips for garnish

Rinse peas thoroughly in colander under cold running water, picking out any debris or blemished peas. Place peas, pork hocks and water in 5-quart Dutch oven.

Add onion, carrots, salt, basil, oregano and pepper to Dutch oven. Bring to a boil over high heat. Reduce heat to medium-low; simmer, uncovered, 1 hour 15 minutes or until peas are tender, stirring occasionally. Stir frequently near end of cooking to keep soup from scorching.

Remove pork hocks; cool. Cut meat into bite-size pieces.

Carefully ladle 3 cups hot soup into food processor or blender; cover and process until mixture is smooth.

Return puréed soup and meat to Dutch oven. (If soup is too thick, add a little water until desired consistency is reached.) Heat through. Ladle into bowls. Garnish, if desired.

Makes 6 servings

234

Split peas, whether green or yellow, are a special variety grown only for drying. Unlike dried beans, split peas do not need to be soaked in water before cooking.

Split Pea Soup

Italian-Style Meatball Soup

½ **pound lean ground beef**
¼ **pound ground Italian sausage**
⅓ **cup fine dry bread crumbs**
1 **egg**
1 **large onion, finely chopped and divided**
½ **teaspoon salt**
4 **cups canned beef broth**
2 **cups water**
1 **can (8 ounces) stewed tomatoes**
1 **can (8 ounces) pizza sauce**
1 **can (15½ ounces) kidney beans, drained**
2 **cups sliced cabbage**
2 **medium carrots, sliced**
½ **cup frozen Italian green beans**

1. Combine beef, sausage, bread crumbs, egg, 2 tablespoons onion and salt in large bowl; mix with hands until thoroughly blended. Shape into 32 (1-inch) meatballs.

2. Brown half the meatballs in large skillet over medium heat, turning frequently and shaking skillet to keep meatballs round. Remove from skillet and drain meatballs on paper towels. Repeat with remaining meatballs.

3. Heat broth, water, tomatoes and pizza sauce in 5-quart Dutch oven over high heat until boiling. Add meatballs, remaining onion, kidney beans, cabbage and carrots. Bring to a boil. Reduce heat to medium-low; simmer, uncovered, 20 minutes. Add green beans; simmer, uncovered, 10 minutes more.

Makes 8 servings

Beef and Pasta Soup

1 tablespoon vegetable oil
½ pound beef round steak, cut into ½-inch cubes
1 medium onion, chopped
3 cloves garlic, minced
4 cups canned beef broth or beef stock
1 can (10¾ ounces) tomato purée
2 teaspoons dried Italian seasoning
2 bay leaves
1 package (9 ounces) frozen Italian green beans
½ cup uncooked orzo or rosamarina (rice-shaped pastas)
   Salt
   Lemon slices and fresh oregano for garnish
   Freshly grated Parmesan cheese (optional)
   French bread (optional)

1. Heat oil in 5-quart Dutch oven over medium-high heat; add beef, onion and garlic. Cook and stir until meat is crusty brown and onion is slightly tender.

2. Stir in broth, tomato purée, Italian seasoning and bay leaves. Bring to a boil over high heat. Reduce heat to medium-low; simmer, uncovered, 45 minutes.

3. Add beans and uncooked pasta. Bring to a boil over high heat. Simmer, uncovered, 8 minutes or until beans and pasta are tender, stirring frequently. Season with salt to taste.

4. Discard bay leaves. Ladle soup into bowls. Garnish, if desired. Serve with freshly grated Parmesan cheese and French bread, if desired. *Makes 5 servings*

Helpful Hint

Italian seasoning is a blend of dried basil, oregano, rosemary and sometimes other seasonings such as marjoram. If Italian seasoning is unavailable, substitute 1 teaspoon dried basil, ¼ teaspoon dried oregano and ¼ teaspoon rosemary.

Beef and Pasta Soup

"Secret Chowder"

1 bag (16 ounces) BIRDS EYE® frozen Pasta Secrets White Cheddar
1 can (10¾ ounces) cream of potato soup
1 cup 1% milk
½ cup water
½ cup cubed cooked lean ham
½ teaspoon dried basil

● In medium saucepan, combine all ingredients.

● Bring to boil over medium-high heat. Reduce heat to medium; cook 15 minutes or until heated through. Add salt and pepper to taste.   *Makes 4 servings*

Cheddar Cheese Chowder: Substitute 1 can Cheddar cheese soup for the cream of potato soup.

Prep Time: 5 minutes
Cook Time: 15 minutes

Wild Rice Soup

½ cup uncooked wild rice
1 pound lean ground beef
1 can (14½ ounces) chicken broth
1 can (10¾ ounces) condensed cream of mushroom soup
2 cups milk
1 cup (4 ounces) shredded Cheddar cheese
⅓ cup shredded carrot
1 packet (.4 ounce) HIDDEN VALLEY® The Original Ranch® Buttermilk Recipe Salad Dressing Mix
Chopped green onions with tops

Cook rice according to package directions to make about 1½ cups cooked rice. In Dutch oven or large saucepan, brown beef; drain off excess fat. Stir in rice, chicken broth, cream of mushroom soup, milk, cheese, carrot and dry salad dressing mix. Heat to a simmer over low heat, stirring occasionally, about 15 minutes. Serve in warmed soup bowls; top with green onions. Garnish with additional green onions, if desired.   *Makes 6 to 8 servings*

Ham and Beer Cheese Soup

   1 cup chopped onion
   ½ cup sliced celery
   2 tablespoons butter or margarine
   1 cup hot water
   1 HERB-OX® chicken flavor bouillon cube *or* 1 teaspoon instant chicken boullion
   3 cups half-and-half
   3 cups (18 ounces) diced CURE 81® ham
   1 (16-ounce) loaf pasteurized process cheese spread, cubed
   1 (12-ounce) can beer
   3 tablespoons all-purpose flour
      Popcorn (optional)

In Dutch oven over medium-high heat, sauté onion and celery in butter until tender. In small liquid measuring cup, combine water and bouillon to make broth; set aside. Add half-and-half, ham, cheese, beer and ¾ cup broth to onion and celery mixture. Cook, stirring constantly, until cheese melts. Combine remaining ¼ cup broth and flour; stir until smooth. Add flour mixture to soup, stirring constantly. Cook, stirring constantly, until slightly thickened. Sprinkle individual servings with popcorn, if desired.   *Makes 8 servings*

241

Hearty Beefy Beer Soup

1 tablespoon vegetable oil
¾ pound round steak, cut into ½-inch cubes
1 large onion, chopped
2 medium carrots, sliced
2 ribs celery, diced
5 cups canned beef broth or beef stock
1 can (12 ounces) beer
¾ teaspoon dried oregano leaves
¼ teaspoon salt
⅛ teaspoon black pepper
1 small zucchini squash, cut into ½-inch cubes
4 ounces mushrooms, sliced
1 can (15 ounces) kidney beans, drained
Fresh herb sprigs for garnish

1. Heat oil in 5-quart Dutch oven over medium heat. Add beef, onion, carrots and celery to hot oil. Cook and stir until meat is no longer pink and carrots and celery are slightly tender.

2. Stir in broth, beer, oregano, salt and pepper. Bring to a boil over high heat. Reduce heat to medium-low; simmer, uncovered, 45 minutes.

3. Stir zucchini, mushrooms and kidney beans into soup. Bring to a boil over high heat. Reduce heat to medium-low; simmer, uncovered, about 5 minutes or until zucchini is tender. Ladle into bowls. Garnish, if desired.   *Makes 6 servings*

242

Hearty Beefy Beer Soup

Potato & Cheddar Soup

2 cups water
2 cups cubed peeled red potatoes
3 tablespoons butter or margarine
1 small onion, finely chopped
3 tablespoons all-purpose flour
   Red and black pepper to taste
3 cups milk
½ teaspoon sugar
1 cup shredded Cheddar cheese
1 cup cubed cooked ham

1. Bring water to a boil in large saucepan. Add potatoes and cook until tender. Drain, reserving liquid. Measure 1 cup, adding water if necessary.

2. Melt butter in saucepan over medium heat. Add onion; cook and stir until tender but not brown. Add flour; season with red and black pepper. Cook 3 to 4 minutes. Gradually add potatoes, reserved liquid, milk and sugar to onion mixture; stir well. Add cheese and ham. Simmer over low heat 30 minutes, stirring frequently. *Makes 12 servings*

Prep Time: 15 minutes
Cook Time: 1 hour

244

Turn a simple soup into a filling supper by serving it in individual bread bowls. Buy or bake small, round loaves of hearty bread, such as Italian or sourdough. Slice a small piece from the top and then remove the inside of the loaf, leaving a 1½-inch shell. Fill with soup and serve.

Potato & Cheddar Soup

Ranch Clam Chowder

¼ cup chopped onion
3 tablespoons butter or margarine
½ pound fresh mushrooms, sliced
2 tablespoons Worcestershire sauce
1½ cups half-and-half
1 can (10¾ ounces) cream of potato soup
¼ cup dry white wine
1 packet (1 ounce) HIDDEN VALLEY® The Original Ranch® Salad Dressing & Seasoning Mix
1 can (10 ounces) whole baby clams, undrained

In 3-quart saucepan, cook onion in butter over medium heat until onion is soft but not browned. Add mushrooms and Worcestershire sauce. Cook until mushrooms are soft and pan juices have almost evaporated. In medium bowl, whisk together half-and-half, potato soup, wine and salad dressing mix until smooth. Drain clam liquid into dressing mixture; stir into mushrooms in pan. Cook, uncovered, until soup is heated through but not boiling. Add clams to soup; cook until heated through. Garnish with chopped parsley.   *Makes 6 servings*

Creamy Vegetable Bisque

1 bag (16 ounces) BIRDS EYE® frozen Broccoli Cuts
2 teaspoons butter or margarine
⅓ cup chopped celery or onion (or a combination)
1 can (10¾ ounces) cream of celery soup
1¼ cups milk or water
1 tablespoon chopped parsley

- Cook broccoli according to package directions; drain.

- Melt butter in saucepan. Add celery; cook 3 to 5 minutes stirring occasionally until tender.

- Blend in broccoli, soup, milk and parsley; cook over medium heat 4 to 5 minutes.
Makes 4 to 6 servings

Prep Time: 2 to 3 minutes
Cook Time: 8 to 10 minutes

Ranch Clam Chowder

Salmon, Corn & Barley Chowder

1 teaspoon vegetable oil
¼ cup chopped onion
1 clove garlic, minced
2½ cups reduced-sodium chicken broth
¼ cup quick-cooking barley
1 tablespoon water
1 tablespoon all-purpose flour
1 can (4 ounces) salmon, drained
1 cup frozen corn, thawed
⅓ cup reduced-fat (2%) milk
½ teaspoon chili powder
¼ teaspoon ground cumin
¼ teaspoon dried oregano leaves
⅛ teaspoon salt
1 tablespoon minced cilantro
⅛ teaspoon black pepper
Lime wedges (optional)

1. Heat oil in medium saucepan over medium heat until hot. Add onion and garlic. Cook and stir 1 to 2 minutes or until onion is tender.

2. Add broth and bring to a boil. Stir in barley. Cover; reduce heat to low. Simmer 10 minutes or until barley is tender.

3. Stir water slowly into flour in cup until smooth. Remove and discard bones and skin from salmon; flake salmon into bite-size pieces.

4. Add corn, salmon and milk to saucepan, stirring to blend. Stir in flour mixture, then chili powder, cumin, oregano and salt. Simmer gently 2 to 3 minutes or until slightly thickened. Stir in cilantro and pepper. Serve with lime wedges, if desired.   *Makes 2 (2¼-cup) servings*

Salmon, Corn & Barley Chowder

Creamy Crab Chowder

1 tablespoon butter or margarine
1 cup finely chopped onions
2 cloves garlic, minced
1 cup finely chopped celery
½ cup finely chopped green bell pepper
½ cup finely chopped red bell pepper
3 cans (13¾ ounces each) chicken broth
3 cups peeled, diced potatoes
1 package (10 ounces) frozen corn
2 cans (6½ ounces each) lump crabmeat
½ cup half-and-half
¼ teaspoon black pepper

Melt butter over medium heat in Dutch oven. Add onions and garlic. Cook and stir 6 minutes or until softened but not browned. Add celery and bell peppers. Cook 8 minutes or until celery is softened, stirring often.

Add broth and potatoes. Bring to a boil over high heat. Reduce heat to low and simmer 10 minutes. Add corn; cook 5 minutes or until potatoes are tender. Drain crabmeat and place in small bowl. Flake to break up large pieces; add to Dutch oven. Stir in half-and-half and pepper. Bring to a simmer. *Do not boil*. Serve hot.

Makes 6 to 8 servings

250

Half-and-half is made of equal parts cream and milk. If it is unavailable, you may substitute whole milk or a combination of whipping cream and milk.

Creamy Crab Chowder

Hearty Pasta and Chick-Pea Chowder

6 ounces uncooked rotini pasta
2 tablespoons olive oil
¾ cup chopped onion
½ cup thinly sliced carrot
½ cup chopped celery
2 cloves garlic, minced
¼ cup all-purpose flour
1½ teaspoons dried Italian seasoning
⅛ teaspoon red pepper flakes
⅛ teaspoon black pepper
2 cans (13¾ ounces each) chicken broth
1 can (19 ounces) chick-peas, rinsed and drained
1 can (14½ ounces) Italian-style stewed tomatoes, undrained
6 slices bacon
    Grated Parmesan cheese

1. Cook rotini according to package directions. Rinse, drain and set aside.

2. Meanwhile, heat oil in 4-quart Dutch oven over medium-high heat until hot. Add onion, carrot, celery and garlic. Cook and stir over medium heat 5 to 6 minutes or until vegetables are crisp-tender.

3. Remove from heat. Stir in flour, Italian seasoning, red pepper flakes and black pepper until well blended. Gradually stir in broth. Return to heat and bring to a boil, stirring frequently. Boil, stirring constantly, 1 minute. Reduce heat to medium. Stir in cooked pasta, chick-peas and tomatoes. Cook 5 minutes or until heated through.

4. Meanwhile, place bacon between double layer of paper towels on paper plate. Microwave at HIGH 5 to 6 minutes or until bacon is crisp. Drain and crumble.

5. Sprinkle each serving with bacon and grated cheese. Serve immediately.

Makes 6 servings (about 7 cups)

Serving Suggestion: Serve with crusty bread, salad greens tossed with Italian dressing, and fruit cobbler.

Prep and Cook Time: 30 minutes

Hearty Pasta and Chick-Pea Chowder

Hearty White Bean Soup

1 tablespoon BERTOLLI® Olive Oil
1 medium onion, chopped
2 medium carrots, sliced
2 ribs celery, sliced
1 clove garlic, crushed
2 cans (19 ounces each) cannelini or white kidney beans, rinsed and drained
1 envelope LIPTON® RECIPE SECRETS® Savory Herb with Garlic Soup Mix
2 cups water
3 cups coarsely chopped escarole or spinach
1 medium tomato, diced
¼ cup crumbled feta cheese (optional)

In 3-quart saucepan, heat oil over medium heat and cook onion, carrots, celery and garlic, stirring occasionally, 5 minutes or until tender. Stir in beans and soup mix blended with water. Bring to a boil over high heat. Reduce heat to low and simmer uncovered 15 minutes or until vegetables are tender. Stir in escarole and tomato and cook 2 minutes or until heated through. Top with cheese. *Makes about 6 cups soup*

254

Pasta e Fagioli

½ cup chopped onion
½ cup sliced carrot
½ cup sliced celery
4 tablespoons extra-virgin olive oil
2 cloves garlic, finely chopped
2 cups reduced-sodium chicken broth or more as needed
1 can (15 ounces) cannellini beans, rinsed and drained
1 can (14½ ounces) Italian plum tomatoes with juices
2 cups packed dark leaves of escarole or Swiss chard, cut into small pieces
1 cup BARILLA® Ditalini or other small pasta shape
1 cup cut green beans (fresh or frozen)
1 cup frozen small lima beans
   Salt and pepper
¼ cup grated Romano cheese, plus more to taste

1. Combine onion, carrot, celery, olive oil and garlic in large broad saucepan. Cover and cook over low heat about 10 minutes until vegetables are tender but not browned.

2. Stir in broth, beans and tomatoes with liquid. Cover and cook about 15 minutes until flavors are blended.

3. Add escarole, ditalini, green beans and lima beans to saucepan. Cook, uncovered, 10 to 12 minutes or until vegetables are very tender and mixture is thick. Add salt and pepper to taste. Stir in cheese. Ladle into bowls; serve with additional cheese.   *Makes 4 to 6 servings*

Ranch Clam Chowder

   3 cans (6½ ounces each) chopped clams
   6 slices bacon, chopped*
   ¼ cup finely chopped onion
   ¼ cup all-purpose flour
  2½ cups milk
   1 packet (1 ounce) HIDDEN VALLEY® The Original Ranch® Salad Dressing & Seasoning Mix
   2 cups frozen cubed O'Brien potatoes
   2 cups frozen corn kernels
   ⅛ teaspoon dried thyme (optional)

*Bacon pieces may be used.

Drain clams, reserving juice (about 1⅓ cups); set aside. Cook bacon until crisp in a large pot or Dutch oven; remove with slotted spoon, reserving ¼ cup drippings.** Set aside bacon pieces. Heat bacon drippings over medium heat in same pot. Add onion; sauté 3 minutes. Sprinkle with flour; cook and stir 1 minute longer. Gradually whisk in reserved clam juice and milk, stirring until smooth. Whisk in salad dressing & seasoning mix until blended. Stir in potatoes, corn and thyme, if desired. Bring mixture just to a boil; reduce heat and simmer 10 minutes, stirring occasionally. Stir in clams; heat through. Sprinkle bacon on each serving.
Makes 4 to 6 servings

**You may substitute ¼ cup butter for the bacon drippings.

Hearty Vegetable Gumbo

    Nonstick cooking spray
½ **cup chopped onion**
½ **cup chopped green bell pepper**
¼ **cup chopped celery**
 2 **cloves garlic, minced**
 2 **cans (about 14 ounces each) no-salt-added stewed tomatoes, undrained**
 2 **cups no-salt-added tomato juice**
 1 **can (15 ounces) red beans, rinsed and drained**
 1 **tablespoon chopped fresh parsley**
¼ **teaspoon dried oregano leaves**
¼ **teaspoon hot pepper sauce**
 2 **bay leaves**
1½ **cups quick-cooking brown rice**
 1 **package (10 ounces) frozen chopped okra, thawed**

256

1. Spray 4-quart Dutch oven with cooking spray; heat over medium heat until hot. Add onion, bell pepper, celery and garlic. Cook and stir 3 minutes or until crisp-tender.

2. Add stewed tomatoes, juice, beans, parsley, oregano, pepper sauce and bay leaves. Bring to a boil over high heat. Add rice. Cover; reduce heat to medium-low. Simmer 15 minutes or until rice is tender.

3. Add okra; cook, covered, 5 minutes more or until okra is tender. Remove and discard bay leaves.
Makes 4 (2-cup) servings

Gumbo is a classic Creole soup or stew. The traditional version consists of combinations of meat, sausage, poultry, seafood, tomatoes and vegetables. This version is meatless. If you wish, you may add 2 cups of cooked chicken or shrimp.

Hearty Vegetable Gumbo

"Dearhearts" Seafood Bisque

2 tablespoons olive oil
1 onion, finely chopped
2 cups chicken broth
1 (9-ounce) package frozen artichoke hearts, thawed
½ cup white wine
1 pound mixed shellfish (raw shrimp, peeled and deveined; raw scallops; or canned crabmeat)
1 cup heavy or whipping cream
2 tablespoons chopped fresh parsley
1 teaspoon salt
½ teaspoon ground nutmeg
¼ teaspoon white pepper

1. Heat oil in large skillet over medium-high heat. Add onion; cook and stir 5 minutes or until softened. Add chicken broth, artichokes and wine. Bring to a boil over medium-high heat. Reduce heat to low. Simmer, covered, 5 to 7 minutes.

2. Process soup in small batches in food processor or blender until smooth. Return soup to saucepan.

3. Stir in shellfish, cream, parsley, salt, nutmeg and pepper. Bring soup just to a simmer over medium heat. Reduce heat to low. Simmer very gently, uncovered, 5 to 10 minutes. *Do not boil.* (Shellfish will become tough if soup boils.) Garnish, if desired.   *Makes 6 servings*

"Dearhearts" Seafood Bisque

Velveeta® Cheesy Baked Potato Soup

¾ cup chopped onion
2 tablespoons butter or margarine
2 cups water
1 can (14½ ounces) chicken broth
2 to 3 large baked potatoes, cubed
   Dash pepper
¾ pound (12 ounces) VELVEETA® Pasteurized Prepared Cheese Product, cut up

1. Cook and stir onion in butter in large saucepan on medium-high heat until tender.

2. Stir in water, broth, potatoes and pepper; heat thoroughly.

3. Add Velveeta; stir on low heat until melted. Serve with bacon bits, BREAKSTONE'S® or KNUDSEN® Sour Cream and chopped fresh parsley, if desired.   *Makes 6 cups*

Prep Time: 15 minutes plus baking potatoes
Cook Time: 15 minutes

Asian Pasta & Shrimp Soup

1 package (3½ ounces) fresh shiitake mushrooms
2 teaspoons Oriental sesame oil
2 cans (14½ ounces *each*) vegetable broth
4 ounces angel-hair pasta, broken into 2-inch lengths (about 1 cup)
½ pound medium shrimp, peeled and deveined
4 ounces snow peas, cut into thin strips
2 tablespoons *French's*® Napa Valley Style Dijon Mustard
1 tablespoon *Frank's*® *RedHot*® Cayenne Pepper Sauce
⅛ teaspoon ground ginger

1. Remove and discard stems from mushrooms. Cut mushrooms into thin strips. Heat oil in large saucepan over medium-high heat. Add mushrooms; stir-fry 3 minutes or just until tender.

2. Add broth and ½ *cup water* to saucepan. Heat to boiling. Stir in pasta. Cook 2 minutes or just until tender.

3. Add remaining ingredients, stirring frequently. Heat to boiling. Reduce heat to medium-low. Cook 2 minutes or until shrimp turn pink and peas are tender.   *Makes 4 servings*

Prep Time: 10 minutes
Cook Time: about 10 minutes

Mama Mia Minestrone Magnifico

   2 tablespoons extra-virgin olive oil
   8 ounces crimini mushrooms, cut into ½-inch pieces (3 cups)
   1 yellow summer squash (6 ounces), cut into ½-inch cubes (1¼ cups)
   ½ small eggplant, cut into ½-inch cubes (1 cup)
   4 ounces green beans, cut diagonally into ½-inch pieces (1 cup)
   6 cups water
   1 (26-ounce) jar NEWMAN'S OWN® Roasted Garlic and Peppers Sauce
   1 cup Burgundy wine
   1 cup uncooked orzo pasta
   1 (15½- to 19-ounce) can white kidney beans (cannellini), drained
   4 medium tomatoes (1 pound), chopped (2 cups)
   4 fresh basil leaves, chopped
   1 tablespoon chopped fresh Italian parsley
   ¾ cup freshly grated Parmesan cheese
   ½ cup pine nuts, toasted

In 12-inch nonstick skillet, heat oil; sauté mushrooms, squash, eggplant and green beans over medium-high heat 10 minutes, stirring constantly, until golden and tender.

Combine water, pasta sauce and wine in 6-quart saucepot and bring to a boil. Add orzo and simmer 10 minutes, stirring occasionally.

Add sautéed vegetables, white beans, chopped tomatoes, basil and parsley; simmer 5 minutes, stirring occasionally.

Serve with Parmesan cheese and pine nuts to sprinkle on top.   *Makes 8 servings*

Hearty One-Pot Chicken Stew

12 TYSON® Individually Fresh Frozen® Boneless, Skinless Chicken
Tenderloins
1 box UNCLE BEN'S CHEF'S RECIPE® Traditional Red Beans & Rice
1 can (14½ ounces) diced tomatoes, undrained
3 new red potatoes, unpeeled, cut into 1-inch pieces
2 carrots, sliced ½ inch thick
1 onion, cut into 1-inch pieces

PREP: CLEAN: Wash hands. Remove protective ice glaze from frozen chicken by holding under cool running water 1 to 2 minutes. Cut into 1-inch pieces. CLEAN: Wash hands.

COOK: In large saucepan, combine chicken, beans and rice, contents of seasoning packet, 2¼ cups water, tomatoes, potatoes, carrots and onion. Bring to a boil. Cover and reduce heat; simmer 20 minutes or until internal juices of chicken run clear. (Or insert instant-read meat thermometer in thickest part of chicken. Temperature should read 170°F.)

SERVE: Serve with hot rolls, if desired.

CHILL: Refrigerate leftovers immediately.   *Makes 4 servings*

Prep Time: 10 minutes
Cook Time: 20 to 25 minutes

If you're hungry for a

hearty, homey stew,

try an old favorite

like Country Chicken

Stew, Hungarian Beef

Goulash or Fruited

Lamb Stew.

Hearty One-Pot Chicken Stew

Curried Turkey Stew with Dumplings

    2 pounds turkey thighs
    1 medium onion, chopped
4¾ cups cold water, divided
    1 teaspoon salt
    1 teaspoon dried thyme leaves
⅛ teaspoon black pepper
¼ cup cornstarch
    1 teaspoon curry powder
    2 cups frozen mixed broccoli, cauliflower and carrots
    1 large tart apple, peeled, cored and coarsely chopped
¾ cup all-purpose flour
    1 tablespoon chopped fresh parsley
1¼ teaspoons baking powder
¼ teaspoon onion salt
    2 tablespoons shortening
¼ cup milk
    Paprika
¼ cup chopped peanuts
    Fresh herb sprigs for garnish

Rinse turkey. Place onion, turkey, 4 cups water, salt, thyme and pepper in 5-quart Dutch oven. Bring to a boil over high heat. Reduce heat to medium-low; simmer, uncovered, 1 hour 45 minutes or until turkey is tender.

Remove turkey from broth and let cool slightly. Remove fat from broth by using large spoon to skim off as much fat as possible. (Or, refrigerate broth several hours and remove fat that rises to surface. Refrigerate turkey if chilling liquid to remove fat.)

Remove turkey meat from bones; discard skin and bones. Cut turkey into bite-size pieces.

Stir together remaining ¾ cup cold water, cornstarch and curry in small bowl until smooth. Stir into broth. Cook and stir over medium heat until mixture comes to a boil and thickens.

Stir in frozen vegetables, turkey pieces and apple. Bring to a boil over high heat, stirring occasionally.

For dumplings, stir together flour, parsley, baking powder and onion salt. Cut in shortening until mixture forms pea-sized pieces. Stir in milk until just combined.

Drop dough in six mounds on stew. Cover and simmer over medium-low heat about 15 minutes or until wooden toothpick inserted into centers of dumplings comes out clean.

Sprinkle dumplings with paprika. Spoon stew into bowls placing dumpling on top of each serving; sprinkle with peanuts. Garnish, if desired.   *Makes 6 servings*

French Country Chicken Stew

¼ **pound sliced bacon, diced**
4 **boneless, skinless chicken breast halves, cut into 1-inch pieces**
1 **medium onion, chopped**
2 **cloves garlic, minced**
1 **teaspoon dried thyme leaves, crushed**
1 **can (14½ ounces) DEL MONTE® Cut Green Beans, drained**
1 **can (15 ounces) kidney beans, drained**
1 **can (14½ ounces) DEL MONTE Original Style Stewed Tomatoes**
   Salt and pepper to taste

265

1. Cook and stir bacon in large skillet over medium-high heat until almost crisp. Add chicken, onion, garlic and thyme.

2. Cook and stir until onion and garlic are soft, about 5 minutes. Pour off drippings.

3. Add remaining ingredients; bring to a boil over high heat. Reduce heat to low. Simmer, uncovered, 10 minutes.   *Makes 4 servings*

Southwest Turkey Tenderloin Stew

  1 package (about 1½ pounds) turkey tenderloins, cut into ¾-inch pieces
  1 tablespoon chili powder
  1 teaspoon ground cumin
 ¼ teaspoon salt
  1 red bell pepper, cut into ¾-inch pieces
  1 green bell pepper, cut into ¾-inch pieces
  1 can (15½ ounces) chili beans in spicy sauce, undrained
  1 can (14½ ounces) chili-style stewed tomatoes, undrained
 ¾ cup chopped red or yellow onion
 ¾ cup prepared salsa or picante sauce
  3 cloves garlic, minced
    Fresh cilantro (optional)

SLOW COOKER DIRECTIONS
Place turkey in slow cooker. Sprinkle chili powder, cumin and salt over turkey; toss to coat. Add red bell pepper, green bell pepper, beans with sauce, tomatoes with juice, onion, salsa and garlic. Mix well. Cover and cook on LOW 5 hours or until turkey is no longer pink in center and vegetables are crisp-tender. Ladle into bowls. Garnish with cilantro, if desired.

Makes 6 servings

For a less spicy stew, substitute chili beans in mild sauce for those in spicy sauce and choose a mild salsa.

Southwest Turkey Tenderloin Stew

Sweet 'n' Sour Turkey Meatball Stew

    2 pounds ground turkey
    ¾ cup dry bread crumbs
    ½ cup chopped onion
    ⅓ cup chopped water chestnuts
    1 clove garlic, minced
    1 egg
    ½ teaspoon salt
    ½ teaspoon ground ginger
    ¼ teaspoon black pepper
    4 tablespoons reduced-sodium soy sauce, divided
    2 tablespoons vegetable oil
    2 cups water
    ¼ cup apple cider vinegar
    ¼ cup sugar
    1 can (20 ounces) pineapple chunks in juice, drained and juice reserved
    1 medium green bell pepper, cut into ½-inch pieces
    1 medium red bell pepper, cut into ½-inch pieces
    Peel from 1 lemon, coarsely chopped
    2 tablespoons cornstarch
    Hot cooked rice (optional)

Combine turkey, bread crumbs, onion, water chestnuts, garlic, egg, salt, ginger, black pepper and 1 tablespoon soy sauce in large bowl; mix well. Shape into meatballs.*

Heat oil in 5-quart Dutch oven over medium heat. Brown meatballs in hot oil. Remove with slotted spoon. Discard fat. Combine water, vinegar, sugar and reserved pineapple juice in Dutch oven. Return meatballs to Dutch oven.

Bring to a boil over high heat. Reduce heat to low. Cover and simmer 20 to 25 minutes. Stir in pineapple, bell peppers and lemon peel. Simmer, uncovered, 5 minutes.

Blend remaining 3 tablespoons soy sauce into cornstarch in small bowl until smooth. Bring meatballs to a boil over medium-high heat; stir in cornstarch mixture. Cook 5 minutes or until mixture thickens, stirring constantly. Serve over rice, if desired.   *Makes 6 servings*

*To quickly shape uniform meatballs, place meat mixture on a cutting board; pat evenly into a large square, one inch thick. With sharp knife, cut meat mixture into 1-inch squares; shape each square into a ball.

Mexican Chicken Stew

1 tablespoon olive oil
1 pound boneless, skinless chicken breasts, cut into ½-inch cubes
1 can (16 ounces) whole-kernel corn, drained
1 can (15 ounces) red kidney beans, undrained
1 can (15 ounces) black beans, drained and rinsed
1 can (4 ounces) chopped green chilies, undrained
1 cup chicken broth
1½ teaspoons McCORMICK® California Style Garlic Powder
1½ teaspoons McCORMICK® Ground Cumin
1 teaspoon McCORMICK® Oregano Leaves
1 teaspoon McCORMICK® Chili Powder
½ cup sliced scallions
Red bell pepper cut into flower shapes to garnish, if desired

1. Heat oil in large skillet over medium-high heat. Add chicken cubes and cook 5 minutes, stirring often. Remove chicken from skillet and set aside.

2. Add remaining ingredients, except scallions and garnish, to skillet and stir to mix well. Heat to a boil. Reduce heat to medium; cover and cook 10 minutes.

3. Stir in reserved chicken and scallions. Cover and simmer 5 to 10 minutes.

4. Spoon into serving bowl and garnish with red bell pepper flowers.   *Makes 6 servings*

269

Scallions, also known as green onioins, are immature onions that are harvested before the bulb has a chance to begin to develop. They are milder in flavor than mature onions.

Chicken and Dumplings Stew

2 cans (about 14 ounces each) fat-free reduced-sodium chicken broth
1 pound boneless skinless chicken breasts, cut into bite-size pieces
1 cup diagonally sliced carrots
¾ cup diagonally sliced celery
1 onion, halved and cut into small wedges
3 small new potatoes, peeled and cut into cubes
½ teaspoon dried rosemary
¼ teaspoon black pepper
1 can (14½ ounces) diced tomatoes, drained *or* 1½ cups diced fresh tomatoes
3 tablespoons all-purpose flour blended with ⅓ cup water

DUMPLINGS
¾ cup all-purpose flour
1 teaspoon baking powder
¼ teaspoon onion powder
¼ teaspoon salt
1 to 2 tablespoons finely chopped fresh parsley
¼ cup cholesterol-free egg substitute
¼ cup low-fat (1%) milk
1 tablespoon vegetable oil

1. Bring broth to a boil in Dutch oven; add chicken. Cover; simmer 3 minutes. Add carrots, celery, onion, potatoes, rosemary and pepper. Cover; simmer 10 minutes. Reduce heat; stir in tomatoes and dissolved flour. Cook and stir until broth thickens.

2. Combine ¾ cup flour, baking powder, onion powder and salt in medium bowl; blend in parsley. Combine egg substitute, milk and oil in small bowl; stir into flour mixture just until dry ingredients are moistened.

3. Return broth mixture to a boil. Drop 8 tablespoons of dumpling batter into broth; cover tightly. Reduce heat; simmer 18 to 20 minutes. Do not lift lid. Dumplings are done when toothpick inserted into centers comes out clean.

Makes 4 servings

Chicken and Dumplings Stew

Country Chicken Stew

       6 slices bacon, diced
       2 leeks, chopped (white part only) (about ½ pound)
       3 shallots, chopped
       1 medium carrot, cut into ¼-inch pieces
  1½ pounds boneless skinless chicken thighs, cut into 1-inch pieces
  1½ pounds boneless skinless chicken breasts, cut into 1-inch pieces
       ½ pound boneless smoked pork butt, cut into 1-inch pieces
       1 Granny Smith apple, cored and diced
       2 cups dry white wine or chicken broth
  1½ teaspoons herbes de Provence, crushed*
       1 teaspoon salt
         Pepper to taste
       2 bay leaves
       2 cans (15 ounces each) cannellini beans or Great Northern beans, drained

*Substitute ¼ teaspoon each rubbed sage, crushed dried rosemary, thyme, oregano, marjoram and basil leaves for herbes de Provence.

272

Cook and stir bacon in 5-quart Dutch oven over medium-high heat until crisp. Add leeks, shallots and carrot; cook and stir vegetables until leeks and shallots are soft. Stir in chicken, pork, apple, wine and seasonings. Bring to a boil over high heat. Reduce heat to low. Cover and simmer 30 minutes.

Stir in beans. Cover and simmer 25 to 30 minutes more until chicken and pork are fork-tender and chicken is no longer pink in center. Remove and discard bay leaves before serving.

Makes 8 to 10 servings

Leeks have a milder flavor than other members of the onion family. To prepare them, trim off the roots and green tops, then remove any withered outer leaves. Leeks collect a lot of dirt between the leaf layers. To clean them, cut the leeks in half lengthwise and rinse them well under cool running water.

Make-Ahead Moroccan Chicken

1 tablespoon olive oil
4 chicken leg quarters, skinned
5 cups water
1 medium onion, cut into chunks
2 medium carrots, cut into chunks
1 cup canned chick-peas, drained
½ cup golden raisins
4 cloves garlic, minced
1 tablespoon minced fresh ginger
2 cinnamon sticks
1½ teaspoons cumin
½ teaspoon turmeric
2 medium zucchini, cut into chunks
2 cups hot cooked couscous

In large, non-stick soup pot, place olive oil over high heat. Add chicken and cook about 10 minutes, turning to brown on all sides. Stir in water, onion, carrots, chick-peas, raisins, garlic, ginger, cinnamon, cumin and turmeric. Bring to simmer, reduce heat and cook for about 20 minutes. Stir in zucchini and simmer an additional 10 minutes. Remove cinnamon sticks. Season with salt and pepper to taste.

Serve in large bowls, over couscous.

Makes 4 to 6 servings

273

Tip: To freeze, transfer Moroccan Chicken to plastic container with tight fitting lid. Let cool, uncovered, for 20 minutes. Refrigerate, uncovered, until cold, about 40 minutes. Cover tightly and freeze until needed.

Tip: To thaw, transfer from freezer to refrigerator 12 to 24 hours before needed. Reheat in a large, covered soup pot over medium-low heat. Bring to simmer and cook for 5 minutes.

*Favorite recipe from **National Chicken Council***

Fruited Lamb Stew

1 pound boneless lamb
2 tablespoons all-purpose flour
½ teaspoon salt
  Dash ground red pepper
2 tablespoons vegetable oil
1 small leek, sliced
3 cups chicken broth
½ teaspoon grated fresh ginger
8 ounces peeled baby carrots
¾ cup cut-up mixed dried fruit (half of 8-ounce package)
½ cup frozen peas
  Black pepper
1⅓ cups hot cooked couscous
  Fresh chervil for garnish (optional)

274

Preheat oven to 350°F. Cut lamb into ¾-inch cubes. Combine flour, salt and red pepper in medium bowl; toss lamb with flour mixture.

Heat oil in 5-quart ovenproof Dutch oven over medium-high heat. Add lamb; brown, stirring frequently. Add leek, chicken broth and ginger to Dutch oven. Bring to a boil over high heat. Cover; bake in oven 45 minutes.

Remove from oven; stir in carrots. Cover and bake in oven 30 minutes or until meat and carrots are almost tender.

Stir fruit and peas into stew. Cover and bake 10 minutes. If necessary, skim off fat with large spoon. Season with black pepper to taste. Serve stew in bowls; top with couscous. Garnish, if desired.
Makes 4 servings

Hungarian Beef Goulash

¼ cup all-purpose flour
1 tablespoon Hungarian sweet paprika
1½ teaspoons salt
½ teaspoon Hungarian hot paprika
½ teaspoon black pepper
2 pounds beef stew meat (1¼-inch pieces)
4 tablespoons vegetable oil, divided
1 large onion, chopped
4 cloves garlic, minced
2 cans (about 14 ounces each) beef broth
1 can (14½ ounces) stewed tomatoes, undrained
1 cup water
1 tablespoon dried marjoram leaves
1 large green bell pepper, chopped
3 cups uncooked thin egg noodle twists
    Sour cream

276

1. Combine flour, sweet paprika, salt, hot paprika and black pepper in resealable plastic food storage bag. Add ½ of beef. Seal bag; shake to coat well. Repeat with remaining beef.

2. Heat 4½ teaspoons oil in Dutch oven over medium heat until hot. Add ½ of beef; brown on all sides. Transfer to large bowl. Repeat with 4½ teaspoons oil and remaining beef; transfer to same bowl.

3. Heat remaining 1 tablespoon oil in same Dutch oven; add onion and garlic. Cook 8 minutes or until tender, stirring often.

4. Return beef and any juices to Dutch oven. Add broth, tomatoes with juice, water and marjoram. Bring to a boil over medium-high heat. Reduce heat to medium-low; cover and simmer 1½ hours or until meat is tender, stirring once.

5. When meat is tender, stir in bell pepper and noodles; cover. Simmer about 8 minutes or until noodles are tender, stirring once. To serve, ladle into 8 soup bowls. Dollop with sour cream.

Makes 8 servings

Hungarian Beef Goulash

Hearty Ground Beef Stew

1 pound ground beef
3 cloves garlic, minced
1 package (16 ounces) Italian-style frozen vegetables
2 cups southern-style hash brown potatoes
1 jar (14 ounces) marinara sauce
1 can (10½ ounces) condensed beef broth
3 tablespoons *French's*® Worcestershire Sauce

1. Brown beef with garlic in large saucepan; drain. Add remaining ingredients. Heat to boiling. Cover. Reduce heat to medium-low. Cook 10 minutes or until vegetables are crisp-tender.

2. Serve in warm bowls with garlic bread, if desired.   *Makes 6 servings*

Prep Time: 5 minutes
Cook Time: 15 minutes

278

Greek Pork Stew

¼ cup olive oil
1 pork tenderloin, cut into ½-inch cubes (about 2½ pounds)
½ pound small white onions, cut into halves
3 cloves garlic, chopped
1¼ cups dry red wine
1 can (6 ounces) tomato paste
1 can (14½ ounces) beef broth
2 tablespoons balsamic vinegar or red wine vinegar
2 bay leaves
1½ teaspoons ground cinnamon
⅛ teaspoon ground coriander
Hot cooked rice (optional)

Heat oil in 5-quart Dutch oven over medium-high heat. Brown half of pork in Dutch oven. Remove with slotted spoon; set aside. Brown remaining pork. Remove with slotted spoon; set aside.

Add onions and garlic to Dutch oven. Cook and stir about 5 minutes or until onions are soft. Return pork to Dutch oven.

Combine wine and tomato paste in small bowl until blended; add to pork. Stir in broth, vinegar, bay leaves, cinnamon and coriander. Bring to a boil over high heat. Reduce heat to low. Cover and simmer 45 minutes or until pork is fork-tender. Remove and discard bay leaves before serving. Serve with rice, if desired.   *Makes 6 to 8 servings*

Harvest Veal Stew

  ⅓ **cup flour**
  2 **teaspoons salt, divided**
  ½ **teaspoon dried tarragon**
1½ **pounds boneless veal shoulder, cut into 1-inch pieces**
  2 **tablespoons olive oil**
  2 **cups chicken broth**
  ½ **cup white wine or water**
  1 **teaspoon TABASCO® brand Pepper Sauce**
  2 **cups cauliflower pieces**
  2 **cups butternut squash pieces (about 1 inch)**
  4 **ounces green beans, cut into 1½-inch pieces**
    Cooked egg noodles, tossed with butter and parsley

279

Combine flour, 1 teaspoon salt and tarragon in medium bowl; toss with veal until well coated. Heat oil in 5-quart saucepan over medium-high heat. Add veal; cook until well browned, turning occasionally. Add chicken broth, wine, TABASCO® Sauce and remaining 1 teaspoon salt; heat to boiling. Reduce heat to low; cover and simmer 45 minutes.

Add cauliflower, squash and green beans to saucepan; heat to boiling over high heat. Reduce heat to low; cover and simmer 15 minutes or until tender, stirring occasionally. Serve stew with noodles.   *Makes 6 servings*

French-Style Pork Stew

1 package (about 6 ounces) long grain and wild rice
1 tablespoon vegetable oil
1 pork tenderloin (16 ounces), cut into ¾- to 1-inch cubes
1 medium onion, coarsely chopped
1 rib celery, sliced
1½ cups chicken broth
2 tablespoons all-purpose flour
½ package (16 ounces) frozen mixed vegetables (carrots, potatoes and peas)
1 jar (4½ ounces) sliced mushrooms, drained
½ teaspoon dried basil leaves
¼ teaspoon dried rosemary
¼ teaspoon dried oregano leaves
2 teaspoons lemon juice
⅛ teaspoon ground nutmeg

1. Prepare rice according to package directions, discarding spice packet, if desired.

2. While rice is cooking, heat oil in large saucepan over medium-high heat until hot. Add pork, onion and celery; cook 5 minutes or until pork is browned. Stir chicken broth into flour until smooth; add to pork mixture. Cook over medium heat 1 minute, stirring constantly.

3. Stir in frozen vegetables, mushrooms, basil, rosemary and oregano; bring to a boil. Reduce heat to low; simmer, covered, 6 to 8 minutes or until pork is tender and barely pink in center. Stir in lemon juice, nutmeg, and salt and pepper to taste. Serve stew over rice.

Makes 4 (1-cup) servings

Prep and Cook Time: 20 minutes

French-Style Pork Stew

Favorite Beef Stew

1½ pounds beef stew meat, cut into ¾-inch cubes
3 tablespoons all-purpose flour
1 teaspoon salt
½ teaspoon black pepper
2 tablespoons vegetable oil
1 cup beef broth
1 can (16 ounces) whole tomatoes, cut-up and undrained
1 clove garlic, minced
1 bay leaf
1 tablespoon Worcestershire sauce
½ teaspoon dried thyme leaves
¼ teaspoon dried basil leaves
2 potatoes, peeled and cut into ½-inch pieces
1 cup frozen pearl onions
2 carrots, cut into ½-inch pieces
2 ribs celery, cut into ½-inch pieces
Onion rings and fresh herb leaves for garnish

1. Place meat in large bowl; sprinkle with flour, salt and pepper. Toss lightly to coat. Heat oil in 5-quart Dutch oven over medium-high heat. Add meat; brown, stirring frequently.

2. Add broth, tomatoes with juice, garlic, bay leaf, Worcestershire, thyme and basil; bring to a boil over high heat. Reduce heat to low; simmer, uncovered, 1½ hours, stirring occasionally.

3. Increase heat to medium. Add potatoes, onions, carrots and celery; heat until boiling. Reduce heat to low; simmer, uncovered, 30 minutes or until meat and vegetables are tender.

4. Ladle into bowls. Garnish, if desired.   *Makes 6 servings*

Favorite Beef Stew

Tuscan-Style Lamb with White Beans

   1 pound large dried lima (butter) beans
   2 tablespoons Lucini Premium Select Extra Virgin Olive Oil
   3 pounds lamb shoulder, cut into large pieces (fat trimmed)
   3 onions, peeled and quartered
   2 carrots, peeled and quartered
  12 large cloves garlic, sliced
   1 cup dry vermouth or red or white wine* (optional)
   3 cups chicken broth
   1 cup chopped celery, with leaves
   2 bay leaves
   2 large sprigs rosemary *or* 1 tablespoon dried rosemary, crumbled
   1 to 2 cups (4 to 8 ounces) shredded JARLSBERG Cheese

*Note: If not using vermouth or wine, increase chicken broth to 4 cups.

Rinse beans; place in large saucepan. Cover with 2 inches water. Bring to a boil over high heat; boil 2 minutes. Remove from heat; cover and let soak 1 hour. Drain beans; discard water. (Or soak beans in cold water overnight, drain and discard water.)

Heat oil in Dutch oven over high heat. Add lamb; cook and stir 10 minutes. Add onions, carrots and garlic; cook and stir 8 minutes, lifting lamb off bottom of pan to let vegetables cook.

Add vermouth, if desired, and cook 3 minutes. Add broth, celery, bay leaves and rosemary; cover and simmer 1½ hours. Add beans and shredded Jarlsberg and continue to simmer 40 minutes to 1 hour until beans are desired firmness. Remove bay leaves and discard before serving.   *Makes 8 servings*

Vermouth is a white wine flavored with herbs and spices. The two most common types are dry vermouth and sweet vermouth. The dry variety is clear in color and can be substituted for white wine in cooking. The sweet variety is a dull red in color and slightly sweet; it is served as a before-dinner cocktail or as an ingredient in a Manhattan.

Herbed Pork and Vegetable Stew

4 boneless pork chops, cut into ¾-inch cubes
2 teaspoons olive oil
⅓ cup flour
2 (14½-ounce) cans beef broth
1 (14½-ounce) can diced tomatoes with garlic and onion
3 bay leaves
1 teaspoon dried marjoram leaves
½ teaspoon hot pepper sauce
¼ teaspoon salt
8 small new potatoes, quartered
1 (16-ounce) package baby carrots
1 (16-ounce) package small frozen pearl onions

Heat oven to 350°F. In a large nonstick skillet heat oil. Cook pork, one half at a time, for 2 to 3 minutes or until browned. Remove pork from skillet, reserving drippings. Transfer pork to a 4-quart casserole. Stir flour into drippings; stir in broth, tomatoes, bay leaves, marjoram, hot pepper sauce and salt. Cook and stir until thickened and bubbly. Stir tomato mixture into the pork. Add potatoes, carrots and onions. Bake, covered, for 55 to 60 minutes or until carrots are crisp-tender, stirring occasionally. Remove bay leaves. To serve, ladle into soup bowls.

Makes 6 servings

*Favorite recipe from **National Pork Board***

285

Pork and Vegetable Stew with Noodles

2 tablespoons vegetable oil
1 pound lean boneless pork, cut into ¾-inch cubes
3 cups beef broth
3 tablespoons chopped fresh parsley, divided
1 can (14½ ounces) stewed tomatoes
1 large carrot, sliced
3 green onions, sliced
2 teaspoons Dijon mustard
¼ teaspoon rubbed sage
⅛ teaspoon black pepper
3 cups uncooked noodles
1 teaspoon butter or margarine
⅓ cup cold water
2 tablespoons all-purpose flour
Apples and parsley for garnish

286

Heat oil in large saucepan over medium-high heat. Add pork; brown, stirring frequently. Carefully add beef broth. Stir in 1 tablespoon chopped parsley, tomatoes, carrot, onions, mustard, sage and pepper. Bring to a boil over high heat. Reduce heat to medium-low; simmer, uncovered, 30 minutes.

Meanwhile, cook noodles according to package directions; drain. Add reserved 2 tablespoons chopped parsley and butter; toss lightly. Keep warm until ready to serve.

Stir cold water into flour in a cup until smooth. Stir into stew. Cook and stir over medium heat until slightly thickened. To serve, spoon noodles onto each plate. Ladle stew over noodles. Garnish, if desired.

Makes 4 servings

Pork and Vegetable Stew with Noodles

Beef and Parsnip Stew

1¼ pounds beef stew meat, cut into ¾-inch cubes
½ cup all-purpose flour
2 tablespoons vegetable oil
4½ cups beef broth
½ cup dry red wine
1 teaspoon salt
½ teaspoon dried Italian seasoning
⅛ teaspoon black pepper
8 ounces peeled baby carrots
2 parsnips, peeled and cut into ⅜-inch slices
¾ cup sugar snap peas

1. Toss beef in flour to coat. Heat oil in large saucepan over medium-high heat. Add beef and remaining flour; brown, stirring frequently.

2. Stir in broth, wine, salt, Italian seasoning and pepper. Bring to a boil over high heat. Reduce heat to medium-low; simmer, uncovered, 1 hour.

3. Add carrots. Cook 15 minutes. Add parsnips. Simmer 8 minutes or until vegetables and meat are tender.

4. Stir in peas. Cook and stir over medium heat until heated through.   *Makes 5 servings*

Parsnips are root vegetables that are shaped like carrots, but they are broader at the top and are ivory in color. They have a distinctive nutty, sweet flavor. While they can be found year round in produce markets, the peak season for parsnips is during the fall and winter months.

Beef and Parsnip Stew

Oyster Corn Stew

40 medium oysters *or* 1 pint shucked fresh oysters including liquor*
   Salt
1 can (15 ounces) cream-style corn
1 cup milk
¼ teaspoon salt
¼ teaspoon celery seeds
   Dash white pepper
4 tablespoons butter or margarine
1 rib celery, chopped
1 cup cream or half-and-half
   Celery leaves and grated lemon peel for garnish

*Liquor is the term used to describe the natural juices of an oyster.

1. Scrub oysters thoroughly with stiff brush under cold running water. Soak oysters in mixture of ⅓ cup salt to 1 gallon water 20 minutes. Drain water; repeat 2 more times.

2. Place on tray and refrigerate 1 hour to help oysters relax.

3. Shuck oysters, reserving liquor. Refrigerate oysters. Strain oyster liquor from bowl through triple thickness of dampened cheesecloth into small bowl; set aside.

4. Place corn, milk, ¼ teaspoon salt, celery seeds and pepper in large saucepan. Bring to a simmer over medium heat; set aside.

5. Melt butter in medium skillet over medium-high heat. Add celery and cook 8 to 10 minutes or until tender. Add reserved oyster liquor; cook until heated through. Add oysters; heat about 10 minutes, just until oysters begin to curl around edges.

6. Add oyster mixture and cream to corn mixture. Cook over medium-high heat until just heated through. *Do not boil.*

7. Serve in wide-rimmed soup bowls. Garnish, if desired. *Makes 6 servings*

Oyster Corn Stew

Jamaican Black Bean Stew

2 cups brown rice
2 pounds sweet potatoes
3 pounds butternut squash
1 large onion, coarsely chopped
1 can (about 14 ounces) vegetable broth
3 cloves garlic, minced
1 tablespoon curry powder
1½ teaspoons ground allspice
½ teaspoon ground red pepper
¼ teaspoon salt
2 cans (15 ounces each) black beans, drained and rinsed
½ cup raisins
3 tablespoons fresh lime juice
1 cup diced tomato
1 cup diced peeled cucumber

292

1. Prepare rice according to package directions. Peel sweet potatoes; cut into ¾-inch chunks to measure 4 cups. Peel squash; remove seeds. Cut flesh into ¾-inch cubes to measure 5 cups.

2. Combine potatoes, squash, onion, broth, garlic, curry powder, allspice, pepper and salt in Dutch oven. Bring to a boil; reduce heat to low. Simmer, covered, 5 minutes. Add beans and raisins. Simmer 5 minutes or just until sweet potatoes and squash are tender and beans are hot. Remove from heat; stir in lime juice.

3. Serve stew over brown rice and top with tomato and cucumber.   *Makes 8 servings*

Jamaican Black Bean Stew

Shrimp Creole Stew

1½ cups raw small shrimp, shelled
1 bag (16 ounces) BIRDS EYE® frozen Farm Fresh Mixtures Broccoli, Cauliflower & Red Peppers
1 can (14½ ounces) diced tomatoes
1½ teaspoons salt
1 teaspoon hot pepper sauce
1 teaspoon vegetable oil

• In large saucepan, combine all ingredients.

• Cover; bring to boil. Reduce heat to medium-low; simmer 20 minutes or until shrimp turn opaque.
Makes 4 servings

Serving Suggestion: Serve over Spanish or white rice and with additional hot pepper sauce for added zip.

294

Hearty Lentil Stew

2 tablespoons BERTOLLI® Olive Oil
3 medium carrots, sliced
3 ribs celery, sliced
1 cup lentils
3 cups water, divided
1 envelope LIPTON® RECIPE SECRETS® Savory Herb with Garlic Soup Mix*
1 tablespoon cider vinegar or red wine vinegar
Hot cooked brown rice, couscous or pasta

*Also terrific with Lipton® Recipe Secrets® Onion-Mushroom or Onion Soup Mix.

In 3-quart saucepan, heat oil over medium heat and cook carrots and celery, stirring occasionally, 3 minutes. Add lentils and cook 1 minute. Stir in 2 cups water. Bring to a boil over high heat. Reduce heat to low and simmer covered, stirring occasionally, 25 minutes. Stir in soup mix blended with remaining 1 cup water. Simmer, covered, for an additional 10 minutes or until lentils are tender. Stir in vinegar. Serve over hot rice.
Makes about 4 servings

Shrimp Creole Stew

Chicken Chili

1 tablespoon vegetable oil
1 pound ground chicken or turkey
1 medium onion, chopped
1 medium green bell pepper, chopped
2 fresh jalapeño peppers,* chopped
1 can (28 ounces) tomatoes, cut up and undrained
1 can (15½ ounces) kidney beans, drained
1 can (8 ounces) tomato sauce
1 tablespoon chili powder
1 teaspoon salt
1 teaspoon dried oregano leaves
1 teaspoon ground cumin
¼ teaspoon ground red pepper
½ cup (2 ounces) shredded Cheddar cheese

*Jalapeño peppers can sting and irritate the skin; wear rubber gloves when handling peppers and do not touch eyes. Wash hands after handling.

Heat oil in 5-quart Dutch oven or large saucepan over medium-high heat. Cook chicken, onion and bell pepper until chicken is no longer pink and onion is crisp-tender, stirring frequently to break up chicken. Stir in jalapeño peppers, tomatoes with juice, beans, tomato sauce, chili powder, salt, oregano, cumin and red pepper. Bring to a boil over high heat. Reduce heat to medium-low; simmer, uncovered, 45 minutes to blend flavors. To serve, spoon into 6 bowls and top with cheese.

Makes 6 servings

If you think all chilis are alike, take a look at this varied collection. From the traditional beef-and-bean variety to chicken, sausage and meatless chilis, they're all here.

Chicken Chili

7-Spice Chili with Corn Bread Topping

    1 pound ground turkey or lean beef
    1 jar (16 ounces) Original or Spicy TABASCO® brand 7-Spice Chili Recipe
    1 can (16 ounces) kidney beans, rinsed and drained
    ¾ cup water
    1 package (12 ounces) corn muffin mix
    1 can (7 ounces) whole kernel corn with sweet green and red peppers, drained
    1 cup (4 ounces) shredded Cheddar cheese

In large skillet, brown turkey; drain. Stir in TABASCO® 7-Spice Chili Recipe, beans and water. Bring to a boil; reduce heat. Simmer 10 minutes.

Divide evenly among 6 (12-ounce) individual ramekins.

Meanwhile, prepare corn muffin mix according to package directions. Stir in corn and cheese until well blended.

Pour about ½ cup muffin mixture over top of each ramekin. Bake at 400°F 15 minutes or until corn bread topping is golden brown.   *Makes 6 servings*

Simple Turkey Chili

    1 pound ground lean turkey
    1 small onion, chopped
    1 can (28 ounces) diced tomatoes, undrained
    1 can (14 ounces) black beans
    1 can (14 ounces) chick-peas, rinsed and drained
    1 can (14 ounces) kidney beans, rinsed and drained
    1 can (6 ounces) tomato sauce
    1 can (4½ ounces) chopped mild green chilies
    1 to 2 tablespoons chili powder, to taste

Cook turkey and onion in Dutch oven over medium-high heat until turkey is no longer pink, stirring with spoon to break up turkey; drain off fat. Stir in all remaining ingredients. Bring to a boil. Reduce heat and simmer, stirring occasionally, about 20 minutes.

Makes 8 servings

Southwest White Chili

SPICE BLEND
- 1 teaspoon McCORMICK® California Style Garlic Powder
- 1 teaspoon McCORMICK® Ground Cumin
- ½ teaspoon McCORMICK® Oregano Leaves
- ½ teaspoon McCORMICK® Cilantro Leaves
- ⅛ to ¼ teaspoon McCORMICK® Ground Red Pepper

CHILI
- 1 tablespoon olive oil
- 1½ pound boneless, skinless chicken breasts, cut into ½-inch cubes
- ¼ cup chopped onion
- 1 cup chicken broth
- 1 can (4 ounces) chopped green chilies, undrained
- 1 can (19 ounces) white kidney beans (cannellini), undrained
- Shredded Monterey Jack cheese
- Sliced scallions, for garnish

299

1. Place all ingredients for spice blend in small dish and stir until well blended. Set aside.

2. Heat oil in 2- to 3-quart saucepan over medium-high heat. Add chicken; cook and stir 4 to 5 minutes. Remove chicken with slotted spoon; cover and keep warm.

3. Add chopped onion to saucepan; cook and stir 2 minutes. Stir in chicken broth, chilies and reserved spice blend. Simmer over low heat 20 minutes.

4. Stir in beans and reserved chicken; simmer, uncovered, 10 minutes.

5. Spoon into serving dish and sprinkle with cheese and scallions.   *Makes 4 servings*

Serving Suggestion: For a quick accompaniment, whip up a batch of cornbread or corn muffins from a mix. For extra flavor, stir grated cheese, chopped scallions or jalapeño peppers or crisply cooked bacon into the batter.

White Bean Chili

Nonstick cooking spray
1 pound ground chicken
3 cups coarsely chopped celery
1½ cups coarsely chopped onions (about 2 medium)
3 cloves garlic, minced
4 teaspoons chili powder
1½ teaspoons ground cumin
¾ teaspoon ground allspice
¾ teaspoon ground cinnamon
½ teaspoon black pepper
1 can (16 ounces) whole tomatoes, coarsely chopped and undrained
1 can (15½ ounces) Great Northern beans, drained and rinsed
2 cups chicken broth

1. Spray large nonstick skillet with cooking spray; heat over medium heat until hot. Add chicken; cook and stir until browned, breaking into pieces with fork. Remove chicken; drain fat from skillet.

2. Add celery, onions and garlic to skillet; cook and stir over medium heat 5 to 7 minutes or until tender. Sprinkle with chili powder, cumin, allspice, cinnamon and pepper; cook and stir 1 minute.

3. Return chicken to skillet. Stir in tomatoes with juice, beans and chicken broth; heat to a boil. Reduce heat to low and simmer, uncovered, 15 minutes. Garnish as desired.

Makes 6 servings

Ground turkey may be substituted for the ground chicken in this recipe. If you wish to lower the amount of fat in the chili, choose a lean ground turkey product that is principally ground turkey breasts.

White Bean Chili

Vegetable-Beef Chili

1 (1-pound) beef top round or chuck steak, cut into ¼-inch cubes
1 tablespoon vegetable oil
1 cup coarsely chopped green bell pepper
½ cup coarsely chopped onion
1 clove garlic, minced
3 to 4 tablespoons chili powder
2 (16-ounce) cans tomatoes, undrained, coarsely chopped
¾ cup A.1.® Original or A.1.® BOLD & SPICY Steak Sauce
1 (17-ounce) can corn, drained
1 (15-ounce) can kidney beans, drained

Brown steak in oil in 6-quart pot over medium-high heat; drain if necessary. Reduce heat to medium; add pepper, onion and garlic. Cook and stir until vegetables are tender, about 3 minutes. Mix in chili powder; cook and stir 1 minute. Add tomatoes with liquid and steak sauce; heat to a boil.

302

Reduce heat. Cover; simmer 45 minutes, stirring occasionally. Add corn and beans; simmer 15 minutes more or until steak is tender. Serve immediately. Garnish as desired.

Makes 6 servings

Hearty Chili

2 pounds BOB EVANS® Original Recipe Roll Sausage
1½ cups chopped onions
1 (1¼-ounce) package chili seasoning
3 cups tomato sauce
3 cups tomato juice
1 (30-ounce) can chili or kidney beans
Hot pepper sauce to taste (optional)

Crumble sausage into large Dutch oven. Add onions. Cook over medium heat until sausage is browned, stirring occasionally. Drain off any drippings; stir in seasoning, then remaining ingredients. Bring to a boil over high heat. Reduce heat to low; simmer, uncovered, 30 minutes. Serve hot. Refrigerate leftovers.

Makes 8 servings

Vegetable-Beef Chili

30-Minute Chili Olé

1 cup chopped onion
2 cloves garlic, minced
1 tablespoon vegetable oil
2 pounds ground beef
1 (15-ounce) can tomato sauce
1 (14½-ounce) can stewed tomatoes
¾ cup A.1.® Steak Sauce
1 tablespoon chili powder
1 teaspoon ground cumin
1 (16-ounce) can black beans, rinsed and drained
1 (11-ounce) can corn, drained
   Shredded cheese, sour cream and chopped tomato, for garnish

Sauté onion and garlic in oil in 6-quart heavy pot over medium-high heat until tender.

Add beef; cook and stir until brown. Drain; stir in tomato sauce, stewed tomatoes, steak sauce, chili powder and cumin.

Heat to a boil; reduce heat to low. Cover; simmer for 10 minutes, stirring occasionally. Stir in beans and corn; simmer, uncovered, for 10 minutes.

Serve hot, garnished with cheese, sour cream and tomatoes.   *Makes 8 servings*

30-Minute Chili Olé

Kahlúa® Turkey Chili Verde

3½ pounds turkey thighs
¼ cup olive oil
2 medium onions, chopped
12 large cloves garlic, peeled and chopped
1 large green bell pepper, chopped
2 tablespoons all-purpose flour
1 (28-ounce) can Italian tomatoes, drained and chopped
1 (14½-ounce) can chicken broth
1 (13-ounce) can tomatillos,* drained and mashed
1½ cups chopped cilantro
4 (7-ounce) cans diced mild green chilies
½ cup KAHLÚA® Liqueur
2 jalapeño chilies, diced**
5 teaspoons dried oregano leaves
2 teaspoons ground coriander seeds
2 teaspoons ground cumin
Salt, freshly ground black pepper and fresh lime juice

*Tomatillos (Mexican green tomatoes) can be found in the ethnic section of large supermarkets.

**Jalapeno chilies can sting and irritate the skin; wear rubber gloves when handling chilies and do not touch eyes. Wash hands after handling chilies.

In large skillet, brown turkey thighs in olive oil over high heat, turning occasionally, about 15 minutes. Transfer to large roasting pan. Set aside. Discard all but ¼ cup drippings in skillet. Add onions, garlic and bell pepper; cook over medium heat until soft, about 10 minutes, stirring frequently. Add flour; cook and stir 3 to 4 minutes. Stir in tomatoes, chicken broth, tomatillos, cilantro, green chilies, Kahlúa®, jalapeño chilies, oregano, coriander and cumin. Bring to boil. Pour over turkey thighs in roasting pan. Cover tightly with heavy-duty foil; bake at 350°F for 1 hour.

Remove from oven; loosen foil. Set turkey aside to cool. When cool enough to handle, remove skin and bones from turkey. Cut meat into ½-inch cubes and place in large saucepan with sauce. Cook over medium heat until heated through. Season to taste with salt, pepper and lime juice. Serve hot; garnish as desired. *Makes about 16 servings*

Sock-it-to-'em Chili

    1 tablespoon vegetable oil
    ¾ pound ground turkey or lean ground beef
    1 (8-ounce) package mushrooms, sliced
    2 medium carrots, peeled and diced
    1 large green bell pepper, seeded and diced
    1 medium onion, diced
    2 cloves garlic, minced
 1½ teaspoons chili powder
    ½ teaspoon ground cumin
    1 (26-ounce) jar NEWMAN'S OWN® Sockarooni Spaghetti Sauce
    2 (15- to 19-ounce) cans black beans, undrained
    1 cup water
    1 medium zucchini, diced

Heat oil in 5-quart Dutch oven over medium-high heat until hot. Add turkey; cook and stir until no longer pink. Add mushrooms, carrots, bell pepper, onion, garlic, chili powder and cumin; cook until onion is tender, stirring frequently.

Stir in Newman's Own® Sockarooni Spaghetti Sauce, beans with their liquid and water; bring to a boil. Reduce heat to low; cover and simmer 20 minutes. Add zucchini; cook over medium-low heat, uncovered, 10 minutes or until zucchini is just tender. Serve hot.

Makes 6 servings

Steak and Black Bean Chili

¾ pound sirloin beef steak
1 teaspoon vegetable oil
1 cup chopped onion
2 cloves garlic, minced
2 cans (15 ounces each) black beans, rinsed and drained
1 can (15 ounces) diced tomatoes, undrained
1 cup chopped green bell pepper
1 cup chopped red bell pepper
1 jalapeño pepper,* minced
1 cube beef bouillon
2 tablespoons chili powder
½ teaspoon sugar
1 cup chopped tomato
⅔ cup sliced green onions with tops
6 tablespoons reduced-fat sour cream

*Jalapeño peppers can sting and irritate the skin; wear rubber gloves when handling peppers and do not touch eyes. Wash hands after handling peppers.

1. Trim fat from steak. Cut steak into ½-inch cubes. Heat oil in large nonstick saucepan over medium heat until hot. Add steak, onion and garlic; cook and stir 5 minutes or until meat is no longer pink. Add beans, diced tomatoes with juice, bell peppers, jalapeño pepper, bouillon, chili powder and sugar. Bring to a boil; reduce heat to low. Simmer, covered, 30 to 45 minutes.

2. Top with chopped tomato, green onions and sour cream. *Makes 6 servings*

Steak and Black Bean Chili

Arizona Pork Chili

1 tablespoon vegetable oil
1½ pounds boneless pork, cut into ¼-inch cubes
  Salt and black pepper (optional)
1 can (15 ounces) black, pinto or kidney beans, drained
1 can (14½ ounces) DEL MONTE® Diced Tomatoes with Garlic & Onion, undrained
1 can (4 ounces) diced green chiles, drained
1 teaspoon ground cumin

1. Heat oil in large skillet over medium-high heat. Add pork; cook until browned. Season with salt and pepper to taste, if desired.

2. Add beans, tomatoes, chiles and cumin. Simmer 10 minutes, stirring occasionally. Serve with tortillas and sour cream, if desired.   *Makes 6 servings*

Prep Time: 10 minutes
Cook Time: 25 minutes

310

Chunky Chili Con Carne

2 pounds ground beef
1 cup chopped onions
1 tablespoon minced fresh garlic
1 can (14.5 ounces) HUNT'S® Whole Tomatoes
1 can (14.5 ounces) beef broth
1 can (6 ounces) HUNT'S® Tomato Paste
3 tablespoons GEBHARDT® Chili Powder
1 teaspoon ground cumin
1 teaspoon salt
½ teaspoon *each:* dried oregano and cayenne pepper
1 can (30 ounces) chili beans

In large pot, brown meat with onions and garlic over medium heat; drain. Stir in tomatoes, broth, tomato paste, chili powder, cumin, salt, oregano and cayenne pepper; reduce heat to low and simmer 20 minutes. Stir in beans; simmer 10 minutes.   *Makes 6 to 8 servings*

Arizona Pork Chili

Southern BBQ Chili

½ pound lean ground beef
1 medium onion, chopped
1 clove garlic, minced
1 can (14½ ounces) DEL MONTE® Diced Tomatoes with Green Pepper & Onion
¼ cup salsa
1 can (15 ounces) barbecue-style beans
1 can (15 ounces) black beans, drained
1 can (8¾ ounces) *or* 1 cup kidney beans, drained

1. Brown meat with onion and garlic in large saucepan; drain.

2. Add tomatoes, salsa and beans. Cover and simmer 15 minutes or until heated through. Top with sour cream and sliced green onions, if desired.   *Makes 6 servings*

Prep Time: 5 minutes
Cook Time: 20 minutes

Spicy Chili with Cornmeal Dumplings

1½ pounds ground beef
1¼ cups finely chopped green bell peppers
½ cup chopped onion
1 clove garlic, minced
½ cup A.1.® Original or A.1.® BOLD & SPICY Steak Sauce
3 large tomatoes, chopped (about 3½ cups)
1 (1¼-ounce) package taco seasoning mix
¼ teaspoon ground cumin
½ teaspoon crushed red pepper flakes
1 (6½-ounce) package corn muffin mix
⅓ cup milk
1 egg
½ cup shredded Cheddar cheese (2 ounces)
¼ cup sliced green onions

Cook beef, green peppers, onion and garlic in large skillet over medium-high heat until beef is browned, stirring occasionally to break up beef. Stir in steak sauce, tomatoes, seasoning mix, cumin and pepper flakes. Heat to a boil; reduce heat. Cover; simmer 10 to 15 minutes to blend flavors.

Meanwhile, mix corn muffin mix according to package directions, using milk and egg. Drop batter into 6 mounds on chili mixture. Cover; simmer 10 to 12 minutes. (Do not lift cover.) Sprinkle with cheese and green onions. Serve immediately.   *Makes 6 servings*

Nell's Chili con Carne

    2 tablespoons vegetable oil
    2 cups diced onions
    1 green bell pepper, seeded and chopped
    3 cloves garlic, minced
    2 pounds lean, coarsely ground beef
    2 cups dried kidney beans, soaked overnight
    1 jar (32 ounces) NEWMAN'S OWN® Spaghetti Sauce
    2 to 3 cups water
    2 to 3 tablespoons chili powder
    1 teaspoon ground cumin
      Salt and black pepper
    1 cup chopped celery
    1 can (8¾ ounces) whole kernel corn, drained
      Sour cream and lime wedges (optional)

313

Heat oil in Dutch oven over medium-high heat. Add onions, bell pepper and garlic; cook and stir until vegetables are tender. Add beef; cook until browned. Add kidney beans, Newman's Own® Spaghetti Sauce, water, chili powder, cumin, and salt and black pepper to taste. Simmer, uncovered, 1 hour, stirring frequently. Add celery and corn and simmer 1 hour. Garnish with sour cream and lime wedges, if desired.   *Makes 8 servings*

Note: Three cups of cooked rice can be substituted for meat to make vegetarian chili.

Texas Chili

4 tablespoons vegetable oil, divided
2 large onions, chopped
3 large cloves garlic, minced
2 pounds boneless sirloin or round steak, cut into ½-inch cubes
1 pound ground beef
2 cans (16 ounces each) tomatoes in purée
1 can (15 to 19 ounces) red kidney beans, undrained
⅓ cup *Frank's*® *RedHot*® Cayenne Pepper Sauce
¼ cup chili powder
2 tablespoons ground cumin
1 tablespoon dried oregano leaves
½ teaspoon ground black pepper

1. Heat 1 tablespoon oil in 5-quart saucepan or Dutch oven. Add onions and garlic; cook 5 minutes or until tender. Transfer to small bowl; set aside.

2. Heat remaining 3 tablespoons oil in saucepan. Add sirloin and ground beef in batches; cook about 15 minutes or until well browned. Drain off fat.

3. Stir in remaining ingredients. Bring to a boil over medium-high heat. Return onions and garlic to saucepan. Simmer, partially covered, 1 hour or until meat is tender. Garnish with shredded Cheddar cheese and chopped green onion, if desired. *Makes 10 servings*

Prep Time: 15 minutes
Cook Time: 1 hour 20 minutes

314

Texas Chili

Texas-Style Chili

Nonstick cooking spray
1 pound lean boneless beef chuck, cut into ½-inch pieces
2 cups chopped onions
5 cloves garlic, minced
2 tablespoons chili powder
1 tablespoon ground cumin
1 teaspoon ground coriander
1 teaspoon dried oregano leaves
2½ cups reduced-sodium beef broth
1 cup prepared salsa or picante sauce
2 cans (16 ounces each) pinto or red beans (or one can of each), rinsed and drained
½ cup chopped fresh cilantro
½ cup nonfat sour cream
1 cup chopped ripe tomatoes

1. Spray Dutch oven or large saucepan with cooking spray; heat over medium-high heat until hot. Add beef, onions and garlic; cook and stir until beef is no longer pink, about 5 minutes. Sprinkle mixture with chili powder, cumin, coriander and oregano; mix well. Add beef broth and salsa; bring to a boil. Cover; simmer 45 minutes.

2. Stir in beans; continue to simmer uncovered 30 minutes or until beef is tender and chili has thickened, stirring occasionally.

3. Stir in cilantro. Ladle into bowls; top with sour cream and tomatoes. Garnish with pickled jalapeño peppers, if desired.
Makes 8 servings

Texas-Style Chili

Winter White Chili

½ pound boneless pork loin *or* 2 boneless pork chops, cut into ½-inch cubes
½ cup chopped onion
 1 teaspoon vegetable oil
 1 (16-ounce) can navy beans, drained
 1 (16-ounce) can chick-peas, drained
 1 (16-ounce) can white kernel corn, drained
 1 (14½-ounce) can chicken broth
 1 cup cooked wild rice
 1 (4-ounce) can diced green chilies, drained
1½ teaspoons ground cumin
 ¼ teaspoon garlic powder
 ⅛ teaspoon hot pepper sauce
   Chopped parsley and shredded cheese

In 4-quart saucepan, sauté pork and onion in oil over medium-high heat until onion is soft and pork is lightly browned, about 5 minutes. Stir in remaining ingredients except parsley and cheese. Cover and simmer for 20 minutes. Serve each portion garnished with parsley and shredded cheese.
Makes 6 servings

Preparation Time: 10 minutes
Cooking Time: 25 minutes

*Favorite recipe from **National Pork Board***

Chilly Day Chili

2 medium onions, chopped
1 green pepper, chopped
2 tablespoons vegetable oil
2 pounds lean ground beef
2 to 3 tablespoons chili powder
1 can (14½ ounces) tomatoes, cut into bite-size pieces
1 can (15 ounces) tomato sauce
½ cup HEINZ® Tomato Ketchup
1 teaspoon salt
¼ teaspoon black pepper
2 cans (15½ ounces each) red kidney beans, partially drained

In large saucepan or Dutch oven, cook and stir onions and green pepper in oil until tender. Add beef; cook until beef is no longer pink, stirring occasionally. Drain excess fat. Stir in chili powder, then add tomatoes, tomato sauce, ketchup, salt and pepper. Simmer, uncovered, 30 minutes, stirring occasionally. Add kidney beans; simmer for an additional 15 minutes.

Makes 8 servings (about 8 cups)

319

Texas Ranch Chili Beans

1 pound lean ground beef
1 can (28 ounces) whole peeled tomatoes, undrained
2 cans (15½ ounces each) chili beans
1 cup chopped onions
1 cup water
1 packet (1 ounce) HIDDEN VALLEY® The Original Ranch® Salad Dressing & Seasoning Mix
1 teaspoon chili powder
1 bay leaf

In Dutch oven, brown beef over medium-high heat; drain off fat. Add tomatoes, breaking up with spoon. Stir in beans, onions, water, salad dressing mix, chili powder and bay leaf. Bring to boil; reduce heat and simmer, uncovered, 1 hour, stirring occasionally. Remove bay leaf just before serving.

Makes 8 servings

Three-Bean Caribbean Chili

1 tablespoon olive oil
1 large onion, chopped
2 cloves garlic, minced
1 jalapeño pepper,* seeded and minced
2 large red or green bell peppers, diced
1 tablespoon plus 2 teaspoons sweet paprika
1 tablespoon plus 2 teaspoons chili powder
2 teaspoons ground cumin
2 teaspoons sugar
½ teaspoon salt
¼ teaspoon ground cloves
1 can (6 ounces) tomato paste
3 cups water
1 can (15 ounces) red kidney beans, drained
1 can (15 ounces) cannellini beans, drained
1 can (15 ounces) black beans, drained
1 tablespoon balsamic vinegar
　Mango Salsa (recipe page 322)
　Hot cooked brown rice

320

*Jalapeño peppers can sting and irritate the skin; wear rubber gloves when handling peppers and do not touch eyes. Wash hands after handling peppers.

1. Heat oil in large saucepan over medium heat until hot. Add onion and garlic; cook and stir 4 minutes. Add jalapeño and bell peppers; cook and stir 5 minutes or until tender.

2. Add paprika, chili powder, cumin, sugar, salt and cloves; cook and stir 1 minute.

3. Stir in tomato paste and water until blended. Bring to a boil over high heat. Reduce heat to low. Cover and simmer 15 minutes. Stir in beans and vinegar; partially cover and simmer 15 minutes or until hot.

4. Meanwhile, prepare Mango Salsa.

5. Serve chili over rice. Top with Mango Salsa. Garnish, if desired.

Makes 6 (1-cup) servings
continued on page 322

Three-Bean Caribbean Chili

Three-Bean Caribbean Chili, continued

Mango Salsa

1 large mango, peeled and cut into ¾-inch cubes
1 small, firm, ripe banana, peeled and cubed
3 tablespoons minced fresh cilantro
1 tablespoon thawed frozen orange juice concentrate
1 teaspoon balsamic vinegar

Combine mango, banana and cilantro in medium bowl. Stir together juice concentrate and vinegar. Pour over fruit; toss.

Makes 1¼ cups

Black Bean Vegetarian Chili

322

1 tablespoon olive oil
2 onions, finely chopped
1 green bell pepper, diced
1 teaspoon ground cumin
1 teaspoon minced garlic
1 to 2 canned chipotle peppers, stemmed and diced, seeds included*
4 cans (15 ounces each) black beans, rinsed and drained
1 can (15 ounces) corn kernels, drained
1 can (15 ounces) diced tomatoes, undrained
1 can (6 ounces) tomato paste plus 3 cans water
½ teaspoon salt
½ teaspoon black pepper
  Sour cream
  Whole wheat flour tortillas (optional)

*Chipotle peppers come in 7-ounce cans packed in adobo sauce. Unused peppers and sauce may be frozen in small plastic bags for later use. Use 1 pepper for mildly spicy chili and 2 peppers for very spicy chili.

1. Heat olive oil in Dutch oven until hot. Reserve ½ cup chopped onions. Add remaining onions and bell pepper to Dutch oven; cook and stir 5 minutes or until soft. Add cumin; cook and stir about 10 seconds. Add garlic; cook and stir 1 minute.

2. Stir in chipotle peppers, black beans, corn, tomatoes with juice, tomato paste, water, salt and black pepper. Bring to a boil. Reduce heat and simmer 30 minutes.

3. Serve with sour cream, reserved onions and whole wheat flour tortillas, if desired.

Makes 8 servings

Rice and Chick-Pea Chili

⅔ cup **UNCLE BEN'S® ORIGINAL CONVERTED® Brand Rice**
1 can (15 ounces) **chick-peas, undrained**
1 can (15 ounces) **diced tomatoes, undrained**
1 can (8 ounces) **diced green chilies**
1 cup **frozen corn**
¼ cup **chopped fresh cilantro**
1 tablespoon **taco seasoning**
½ cup (2 ounces) **shredded reduced-fat Cheddar cheese**

1. In medium saucepan, bring 1¾ cups water and rice to a boil. Cover, reduce heat and simmer 15 minutes.

2. Add remaining ingredients except cheese. Cook over low heat 10 minutes. Serve in bowls sprinkled with cheese.

Makes 4 servings

323

Helpful Hint

To round out the meal, serve this hearty vegetarian chili with fruit and corn bread fresh from the oven.

Chili with Beans and Corn

1 (16-ounce) can black-eyed peas or cannellini beans, rinsed and drained
1 (16-ounce) can kidney or navy beans, rinsed and drained
1 (15-ounce) can whole tomatoes, chopped and drained
1 onion, chopped
1 cup canned or frozen corn
1 cup water
½ cup chopped green onions
½ cup tomato paste
¼ cup diced jalapeño peppers*
1 tablespoon chili powder
1 teaspoon ground cumin
1 teaspoon prepared mustard
½ teaspoon dried oregano leaves

*Jalapeño peppers can sting and irritate the skin; wear rubber gloves when handling peppers and do not touch eyes. Wash hands after handling peppers.

324

SLOW COOKER DIRECTIONS
Combine all ingredients in slow cooker. Cover and cook on LOW 8 to 10 hours or on HIGH 4 to 5 hours.   *Makes 6 to 8 servings*

This vegetarian chili is easy to assemble. Simply combine all ingredients in a slow cooker in the morning and the chili will be ready for dinner eight hours later. Complete the meal with hot bread and a simple dessert.

Chili with Beans and Corn

Turkey Vegetable Chili Mac

Nonstick cooking spray
¾ pound ground turkey breast
½ cup chopped onion
2 cloves garlic, minced
1 can (about 15 ounces) black beans, rinsed and drained
1 can (14½ ounces) Mexican-style stewed tomatoes, undrained
1 can (14½ ounces) no-salt-added diced tomatoes, undrained
1 cup frozen corn
1 teaspoon Mexican seasoning
½ cup uncooked elbow macaroni
⅓ cup reduced-fat sour cream

On the days you

want lighter fare,

choose one of these

recipes. You'll find a

fabulous assortment

of casseroles, skillets,

slow cooker dishes

and more.

1. Spray large nonstick saucepan or Dutch oven with cooking spray; heat over medium heat until hot. Add turkey, onion and garlic; cook 5 minutes or until turkey is no longer pink, stirring to separate meat.

2. Stir beans, tomatoes with juice, corn and Mexican seasoning into saucepan; bring to a boil over high heat. Cover; reduce heat to low. Simmer 15 minutes, stirring occasionally.

3. Meanwhile, cook pasta according to package directions, omitting salt. Rinse and drain pasta; stir into saucepan. Simmer, uncovered, 2 to 3 minutes or until heated through.

4. Top each serving with dollop of sour cream. Garnish as desired.

Makes 6 servings

Nutrients per Serving: Calories: 236 (21% of Calories from Fat), Total Fat: 6 g, Saturated Fat: 1 g, Cholesterol: 25 mg, Protein: 17 g, Carbohydrate: 34 g, Sodium: 445 mg, Fiber: 6 g

Turkey Vegetable Chili Mac

20 Minute Chicken & Brown Rice Pilaf

1 tablespoon vegetable oil
4 boneless skinless chicken breast halves
1 can (10½ ounces) condensed chicken broth
½ cup water
1 cup sliced fresh mushrooms
1 small onion, chopped
1 cup frozen peas
2 cups MINUTE® Brown Rice, uncooked

HEAT oil in skillet. Add chicken; cook until browned. Remove chicken.

ADD chicken broth and water to skillet; stir. Bring to boil.

STIR in mushrooms, onion, peas and rice. Top with chicken; cover. Cook on low heat 5 minutes or until chicken is cooked through. Let stand 5 minutes.   *Makes 4 servings*

Take a Shortcut: Omit oil. Substitute 1 package (6 ounces) LOUIS RICH® Grilled Chicken Breast Strips for the cooked chicken breasts. Bring chicken broth and water to a boil in large skillet. Stir in chicken breast strips with the mushrooms, onions, peas and rice. Cook over low heat until mixture is thoroughly heated, stirring occasionally.

Prep/Cook Time: 20 minutes

Nutrients per Serving: Calories: 500 (18% of Calories from Fat), Total Fat: 10 g, Saturated Fat: 2 g, Cholesterol: 90 mg, Protein: 45 g, Carbohydrate: 55 g, Sodium: 780 mg, Fiber: 5 g

328

Chipotle Tamale Pie

¾ **pound ground turkey breast or lean ground beef**
 1 **cup chopped onion**
¾ **cup diced green bell pepper**
¾ **cup diced red bell pepper**
 4 **cloves garlic, minced**
 2 **teaspoons ground cumin**
 1 **can (15 ounces) pinto or red beans, rinsed and drained**
 1 **can (8 ounces) no-salt-added stewed tomatoes, undrained**
 2 **canned chipotle chilies in adobo sauce, minced (about 1 tablespoon)**
 1 **to 2 teaspoons adobo sauce from canned chilies (optional)**
 1 **cup (4 ounces) low-sodium reduced-fat shredded Cheddar cheese**
½ **cup chopped fresh cilantro**
 1 **package (8½ ounces) corn bread mix**
⅓ **cup low-fat (1%) milk**
 1 **large egg white**

1. Preheat oven to 400°F.

2. Cook turkey, onion, bell peppers and garlic in large nonstick skillet over medium-high heat 8 minutes or until turkey is no longer pink, stirring occasionally. Drain fat; sprinkle mixture with cumin.

3. Add beans, tomatoes with juice, chilies and adobo sauce; bring to a boil over high heat. Reduce heat to medium; simmer, uncovered, 5 minutes. Remove from heat; stir in cheese and cilantro.

4. Spray 8-inch square baking dish with nonstick cooking spray. Spoon turkey mixture evenly into prepared dish, pressing down to compact mixture.

5. Combine corn bread mix, milk and egg white in medium bowl; mix just until dry ingredients are moistened. Spoon batter evenly over turkey mixture to cover completely.

6. Bake 20 to 22 minutes or until corn bread is golden brown. Let stand 5 minutes before serving. *Makes 6 servings*

Nutrients per Serving: Calories: 396 (23% of Calories from Fat), Total Fat: 10 g, Saturated Fat: 3 g, Cholesterol: 32 mg, Protein: 26 g, Carbohydrate: 52 g, Sodium: 733 mg, Fiber: 2 g

330

Chipotle Tamale Pie

Chunky Chicken Stew

1 teaspoon olive oil
1 small onion, chopped
1 cup thinly sliced carrots
1 cup fat-free reduced-sodium chicken broth
1 can (14½ ounces) no-salt-added diced tomatoes, undrained
1 cup diced cooked chicken breast
3 cups sliced kale or baby spinach leaves

1. Heat oil in large saucepan over medium-high heat. Add onion; cook and stir about 5 minutes or until golden brown. Stir in carrots, then broth; bring to a boil.

2. Reduce heat and simmer uncovered 5 minutes. Add tomatoes; simmer 5 minutes or until carrots are tender. Add chicken; heat through. Add kale, stirring until kale is wilted. Simmer 1 minute. Ladle into soup bowls. *Makes 2 servings*

Nutrients per Serving: Calories: 274 (21% of Calories from Fat), Total Fat: 6 g, Saturated Fat: 1 g, Cholesterol: 0 mg, Protein: 30 g, Carbohydrate: 25 g, Sodium: 209 mg, Fiber: 7 g

Turkey Tetrazzini

2 tablespoons cornstarch
1¼ cups skim milk
¾ cup turkey broth or chicken bouillon
½ teaspoon salt
½ teaspoon garlic powder
⅛ teaspoon pepper
2 cups cooked turkey, cut into ½-inch cubes
4 ounces spaghetti, cooked according to package instructions and drained
1 can (4 ounces) mushrooms, drained
1 jar (2 ounces) chopped pimiento, drained
¼ cup grated Parmesan cheese
2 tablespoons dry white wine
2 tablespoons sliced almonds

1. Preheat oven to 375°F.

2. In 3-quart saucepan, over medium heat, combine cornstarch, milk, broth, salt, garlic powder and pepper. Bring mixture to boil, stirring constantly. Remove from heat and stir in turkey, spaghetti, mushrooms, pimiento, cheese and wine.

3. Pour turkey mixture into lightly greased 9-inch square casserole dish. Top with almonds. Bake 25 minutes or until mixture bubbles and top is browned.   *Makes 4 servings*

Favorite recipe from **National Turkey Federation**

Nutrients per Serving: Calories: 320 (19% of Calories from Fat), Total Fat: 7 g, Saturated Fat: 2 g, Cholesterol: 59 mg, Protein: 30 g, Carbohydrate: 32 g, Sodium: 541 mg, Fiber: 2 g

Cajun Chicken Bayou

2 cups water
1 can (10 ounces) diced tomatoes and green chilies, undrained
1 box UNCLE BEN'S CHEF'S RECIPE® Traditional Red Beans & Rice
3 TYSON® Individually Fresh Frozen® Boneless, Skinless Chicken Breasts

COOK: CLEAN: Wash hands. In large skillet, combine water, tomatoes, beans and rice, and contents of seasoning packet; mix well. Add chicken. Bring to a boil. Cover, reduce heat; simmer 30 to 35 minutes or until internal juices of chicken run clear. (Or insert instant-read meat thermometer in thickest part of chicken. Temperature should read 170°F.)

SERVE: Serve with sliced avocados and whole wheat rolls, if desired.

CHILL: Refrigerate leftovers immediately.   *Makes 3 servings*

Prep Time: none
Cook Time: 35 minutes

Nutrients per Serving: Calories: 406 (13% of Calories from Fat), Total Fat: 6 g, Saturated Fat: 2 g, Cholesterol: 70 mg, Protein: 35 g, Carbohydrate: 56 g, Sodium: 1321 mg, Fiber: 2 g

333

Skillet Chicken Soup

¾ **pound boneless skinless chicken breasts or thighs, cut into ¾-inch pieces**
 1 **teaspoon paprika**
½ **teaspoon salt**
¼ **teaspoon black pepper**
 2 **teaspoons vegetable oil**
 1 **large onion, chopped**
 1 **red bell pepper, cut into ½-inch pieces**
 3 **cloves garlic, minced**
 1 **can (19 ounces) cannellini beans or small white beans, rinsed and drained**
 1 **cup fat-free, reduced-sodium chicken broth**
 3 **cups sliced savoy or napa cabbage**
½ **cup fat-free herb-flavored croutons, slightly crushed**

1. Toss chicken with paprika, salt and black pepper in medium bowl until coated.

2. Heat oil in large, deep nonstick skillet over medium-high heat until hot. Add chicken, onion, bell pepper and garlic. Cook until chicken is no longer pink, stirring frequently.

3. Add beans and broth; bring to simmer. Cover and simmer 5 minutes or until chicken is cooked through. Stir in cabbage; cover and simmer 3 additional minutes or until cabbage is wilted. Ladle into shallow bowls; top with crushed croutons.   *Makes 4 servings*

Nutrients per Serving: Calories: 284 (16% of Calories from Fat), Total Fat: 5 g, Saturated Fat: 1 g, Cholesterol: 52 mg, Protein: 28 g, Carbohydrate: 30 g, Sodium: 721 mg, Fiber: 8 g

Skillet Chicken Soup

Low Fat Turkey Bacon Frittata

1 package (12 ounces) BUTTERBALL® Turkey Bacon, heated and chopped
6 ounces uncooked angel hair pasta, broken
2 teaspoons olive oil
1 red bell pepper, cut into thin strips
1 small onion, sliced
4 containers (4 ounces each) egg substitute
1 container (5 ounces) fat-free ricotta cheese
1 cup (4 ounces) shredded fat-free mozzarella cheese
1 cup (4 ounces) shredded reduced-fat Swiss cheese
½ teaspoon salt
½ teaspoon black pepper
1 package (10 ounces) frozen spinach, thawed and squeezed dry

Cook and drain pasta. Heat oil in large skillet over medium heat until hot. Cook and stir bell pepper and onion until tender. Combine egg substitute, cheeses, salt, pepper and cooked pasta in large bowl. Add vegetables, spinach and turkey bacon. Spray 10-inch quiche dish with nonstick cooking spray; pour mixture into dish. Bake in preheated 350°F oven 30 minutes. Cut into wedges. Serve with spicy salsa, if desired. *Makes 8 servings*

Preparation Time: 15 minutes plus baking time

Nutrients per Serving: Calories: 280 (29% of Calories from Fat), Total Fat: 9 g, Saturated Fat: 2 g, Cholesterol: 63 mg, Protein: 12 g, Carbohydrate: 29 g, Sodium: 780 mg, Fiber: 3 g

336

Low Fat Turkey Bacon Frittata

Festive Skillet Fajitas

1½ pounds boneless, skinless chicken breasts, cut into ½-inch strips
1 medium onion, cut into thin wedges
2 cloves garlic, minced
1 tablespoon vegetable oil
½ teaspoon ground cumin
1 can (14½ ounces) DEL MONTE® Zesty Diced Tomatoes with Jalapeño Peppers
1 can (7 ounces) whole green chiles, drained and cut into strips
8 flour tortillas, warmed

1. Brown chicken with onion and garlic in oil in large skillet over medium-high heat.

2. Stir in cumin, tomatoes and chiles; heat through.

3. Fill warmed tortillas with chicken mixture. Garnish with sour cream, avocado or guacamole, cilantro and lime wedges, if desired. Serve immediately.   *Makes 6 to 8 servings*

Prep Time: 10 minutes
Cook Time: 10 minutes

338

Nutrients per Serving: Calories: 334 (24% of Calories from Fat), Total Fat: 9 g, Saturated Fat: 2 g, Cholesterol: 69 mg, Protein: 30 g, Carbohydrate: 32 g, Sodium: 233 mg, Fiber: 4 g

Black Bean and Turkey Stew

3 cans (15 ounces each) black beans, drained and rinsed
1½ cups chopped onions
1½ cups fat-free reduced-sodium chicken broth
1 cup sliced celery
1 cup chopped red bell pepper
4 cloves garlic, minced
1½ teaspoons dried oregano
¾ teaspoon ground coriander
½ teaspoon ground cumin
¼ teaspoon ground red pepper
6 ounces cooked turkey sausage, thinly sliced

SLOW COOKER DIRECTIONS

1. Combine all ingredients, except sausage, in slow cooker. Cover and cook on LOW 6 to 8 hours.

2. Transfer about 1½ cups bean mixture from slow cooker to blender or food processor; purée bean mixture. Return to slow cooker. Stir in sausage. Cover and cook on LOW an additional 10 to 15 minutes.   *Makes 6 servings*

Nutrients per Serving: Calories: 264 (15% of Calories from Fat), Total Fat: 5 g, Saturated Fat: 1 g, Cholesterol: 18 mg, Protein: 16 g, Carbohydrate: 42 g, Sodium: 1370 mg, Fiber: 14 g

Garlic Herb Chicken and Rice Skillet

4 boneless, skinless chicken breasts (about 1 pound)
1¾ cups water
1 box UNCLE BEN'S® COUNTRY INN® Chicken Flavored Rice
2 cups frozen broccoli, carrots and cauliflower
¼ cup garlic and herb flavored soft spreadable cheese

1. In large skillet, combine chicken, water and contents of seasoning packet. Bring to a boil. Reduce heat; cover and simmer 10 minutes.

2. Add rice, vegetables and cheese. Cook covered 10 to 15 minutes or until chicken is no longer pink in center. Remove from heat; let stand 5 minutes or until liquid is absorbed.

Makes 4 servings

Nutrients per Serving: Calories: 331 (14% of Calories from Fat), Total Fat: 5 g, Saturated Fat: 2 g, Cholesterol: 74 mg, Protein: 31 g, Carbohydrate: 39 g, Sodium: 955 mg, Fiber: 3 g

Chicken Gumbo

2 tablespoons all-purpose flour
2 teaspoons blackened seasoning mix or Creole seasoning mix
12 ounces boneless skinless chicken thighs, cut into ¾-inch pieces
2 teaspoons olive oil
1 large onion, coarsely chopped
½ cup sliced celery
2 teaspoons minced garlic
1 can (about 14 ounces) reduced-sodium chicken broth
1 can (14½ ounces) no-salt-added stewed tomatoes, undrained
1 large green bell pepper, cut into chunks
1 teaspoon filé powder (optional)
2 cups hot cooked rice
2 tablespoons chopped fresh parsley

1. Combine flour and blackened seasoning mix in large resealable plastic food storage bag. Add chicken; toss to coat. Heat oil in large deep nonstick skillet or saucepan over medium heat. Add chicken to skillet; sprinkle with any remaining flour mixture. Cook and stir 3 minutes. Add onion, celery and garlic; cook and stir 3 minutes.

2. Add chicken broth, tomatoes with juice and bell pepper; bring to a boil. Reduce heat; cover and simmer 20 minutes or until vegetables are tender. Uncover; simmer 5 to 10 minutes or until sauce is slightly reduced. Remove from heat; stir in filé powder, if desired. Ladle into shallow bowls; top with rice and parsley.   *Makes 4 (1½-cup) servings*

Note: Filé powder, made from dried sassafras leaves, thickens and adds flavors to gumbos. Look for it in the herb and spice section of your supermarket.

Prep Time: 15 minutes
Cook Time: 40 minutes

Nutrients per Serving: Calories: 306 (27% of Calories from Fat), Total Fat: 9 g, Saturated Fat: 2 g, Cholesterol: 46 mg, Protein: 18 g, Carbohydrate: 38 g, Sodium: 302 mg, Fiber: 3 g

Pork Chops with Jalapeño-Pecan Cornbread Stuffing

6 boneless loin pork chops, 1 inch thick (1½ pounds)
Nonstick cooking spray
¾ cup chopped onion
¾ cup chopped celery
½ cup coarsely chopped pecans
½ medium jalapeño pepper,* seeded and chopped
1 teaspoon rubbed sage
½ teaspoon dried rosemary
⅛ teaspoon black pepper
4 cups unseasoned cornbread stuffing mix
1¼ cups reduced-sodium chicken broth
1 egg, lightly beaten

*Jalapeño peppers can sting and irritate the skin; wear rubber gloves when handling peppers and do not touch eyes. Wash hands after handling peppers.

SLOW COOKER DIRECTIONS

Trim excess fat from pork and discard. Spray large skillet with nonstick cooking spray; heat over medium heat. Add pork; cook 10 minutes or until browned on all sides. Remove; set aside. Add onion, celery, pecans, jalapeño pepper, sage, rosemary and pepper to skillet. Cook 5 minutes or until onion and celery are tender; set aside.

Combine cornbread stuffing mix, vegetable mixture and broth in medium bowl. Stir in egg. Spoon stuffing mixture into slow cooker. Arrange pork on top. Cover and cook on LOW about 5 hours or until pork is tender and barely pink in center. Serve with vegetable salad, if desired.

Makes 6 servings

Note: If you prefer a more moist dressing, increase the chicken broth to 1½ cups.

Nutrients per Serving: Calories: 379 (37% of Calories from Fat), Total Fat: 16 g, Saturated Fat: 4 g, Cholesterol: 87 mg, Protein: 26 g, Carbohydrate: 33 g, Sodium: 586 mg, Fiber: 7 g

Pork Chop with Jalapeño-Pecan Cornbread Stuffing

Beef and Parsnip Stroganoff

1 cube beef bouillon

¾ cup boiling water

¾ pound well-trimmed boneless top round beef steak, 1 inch thick
   Nonstick olive oil cooking spray

2 cups cubed peeled parsnips or potatoes*

1 medium onion, halved and thinly sliced

¾ pound mushrooms, sliced

2 teaspoons minced garlic

¼ teaspoon black pepper

¼ cup water

1 tablespoon plus 1½ teaspoons all-purpose flour

3 tablespoons reduced-fat sour cream

1½ teaspoons Dijon mustard

¼ teaspoon cornstarch

1 tablespoon chopped fresh parsley

4 ounces cholesterol-free wide noodles, cooked without salt, drained and kept hot

*If using potatoes, cut into 1-inch chunks and do not sauté.

SLOW COOKER DIRECTIONS

1. Dissolve bouillon cube in ¾ cup boiling water; cool. Meanwhile, cut steak into 2×½-inch strips. Spray large nonstick skillet with cooking spray; heat over high heat. Cook and stir beef 4 minutes or until meat begins to brown. Transfer beef and juices to slow cooker.

2. Spray same skillet with cooking spray; heat over high heat. Add parsnips and onion; cook and stir until browned, about 4 minutes. Add mushrooms, garlic and pepper; cook and stir until mushrooms are tender, about 5 minutes. Transfer mushroom mixture to slow cooker.

3. Stir ¼ cup water into flour in small bowl until smooth. Stir flour mixture into cooled bouillon. Add to slow cooker; stir until blended. Cook, covered, on LOW 4½ to 5 hours or until beef and parsnips are tender.

4. Turn off slow cooker. Remove beef and vegetables with slotted spoon to large bowl; reserve cooking liquid. Blend sour cream, mustard and cornstarch in medium bowl. Gradually add reserved liquid to sour cream mixture; stir well to blend. Stir sour cream mixture into beef mixture. Sprinkle with parsley; serve over noodles. *Makes 4 servings*

Nutrients per Serving: Calories: 347 (15% of Calories from Fat), Total Fat: 6 g, Saturated Fat: 2 g, Cholesterol: 46 mg, Protein: 28 g, Carbohydrate: 46 g, Sodium: 242 mg, Fiber: 5 g

Beef Stew in Red Wine

1½ pounds boneless beef round, cut Into 1-Inch cubes
1½ cups dry red wine
2 teaspoons olive oil
  Peel of half an orange
2 large cloves garlic, thinly sliced
1 bay leaf
½ teaspoon dried thyme leaves
⅛ teaspoon black pepper
8 ounces fresh mushrooms, quartered
8 sun-dried tomatoes, quartered
1 can (about 14 ounces) fat-free, reduced-sodium beef broth
6 small potatoes, unpeeled, cut into wedges
1 cup baby carrots
1 cup fresh pearl onions, outer skins removed
1 tablespoon cornstarch mixed with 2 tablespoons water

1. Combine beef, wine, oil, orange peel, garlic, bay leaf, thyme and pepper in large glass bowl. Refrigerate, covered, at least 2 hours or overnight.

2. Place beef mixture, mushrooms and tomatoes in large nonstick skillet or Dutch oven. Add enough beef broth to just cover ingredients. Bring to a boil over high heat. Cover; reduce heat to low. Simmer 1 hour. Add potatoes, carrots and onions; cover and cook 20 to 25 minutes or until vegetables are tender and meat is no longer pink. Remove meat and vegetables from skillet with slotted spoon; cover and set aside. Discard orange peel and bay leaf.

3. Stir cornstarch mixture into sauce in skillet. Increase heat to medium; cook and stir until sauce is slightly thickened. Return meat and vegetables to sauce; heat thoroughly.

Makes 6 servings

345

Nutrients per Serving: Calories: 313 (16% of Calories from Fat), Total Fat: 6 g, Saturated Fat: 1 g, Cholesterol: 55 mg, Protein: 26 g, Carbohydrate: 31 g, Sodium: 304 mg, Fiber: 3 g

Beef & Bean Burritos

Nonstick cooking spray
½ **pound beef round steak, cut into ½-inch pieces**
3 **cloves garlic, minced**
1 **can (about 15 ounces) pinto beans, rinsed and drained**
1 **can (4 ounces) diced mild green chilies, drained**
¼ **cup finely chopped fresh cilantro**
6 **(6-inch) flour tortillas, warmed**
½ **cup (2 ounces) shredded reduced-fat Cheddar cheese**

1. Spray nonstick skillet with cooking spray; heat over medium heat until hot. Add steak and garlic; cook and stir 5 minutes or until steak is cooked to desired doneness.

2. Stir beans, chilies and cilantro into skillet; cook and stir 5 minutes or until heated through.

3. Spoon steak mixture evenly down center of each tortilla; sprinkle cheese evenly over each tortilla. Fold bottom end of tortilla over filling; roll to enclose. Garnish with salsa and nonfat sour cream, if desired.   *Makes 6 servings*

346

Nutrients per Serving: Calories: 278 (22% of Calories from Fat), Total Fat: 7 g, Saturated Fat: 2 g, Cholesterol: 31 mg, Protein: 19 g, Carbohydrate: 36 g, Sodium: 956 mg, Fiber: 1 g

 *Helpful Hint*

To warm tortillas, stack them, then loosely wrap them in plastic wrap. Microwave at HIGH for about 30 seconds or until tortillas are warm.

Basil Pork & Green Bean Stew

    1 package (9 ounces) frozen cut green beans
3½ cups peeled red potatoes cut into ½-inch cubes
    1 pound trimmed pork tenderloin, cut into 1-inch cubes
    1 cup no-sugar-added prepared meatless spaghetti sauce
    ½ teaspoon salt
    1 tablespoon chopped fresh basil *or* 1 teaspoon dried basil leaves
    ¼ cup grated Parmesan cheese

MICROWAVE DIRECTIONS

1. Place beans in 10- to 12-inch microwavable casserole. Microwave, covered, at HIGH 2 minutes. Drain in colander.

2. Using same dish, microwave potatoes, covered, at HIGH 3 minutes. Stir in pork, beans, spaghetti sauce and salt. Microwave at HIGH 10 minutes, stirring halfway through. Stir in basil. Microwave 5 to 7 minutes or until potatoes are tender and meat is no longer pink in center. Serve with cheese.   *Makes 6 servings*

348

Nutrients per Serving: Calories: 274 (13% of Calories from Fat), Total Fat: 4 g, Saturated Fat: 2 g, Cholesterol: 46 mg, Protein: 21 g, Carbohydrate: 39 g, Sodium: 504 mg, Fiber: 6 g

Pork tenderloin is the best choice for this recipe, because it is lower in fat than other pork cuts, such as chops and loin roast.

Basil Pork & Green Bean Stew

Zesty Lamb Taco Skillet

    1 tablespoon vegetable or olive oil
    1 clove garlic, minced
    1 pound boneless lamb (leg or shoulder), cut into ⅛-inch strips
 1½ cans (21 ounces) reduced sodium beef broth
 1½ cans (12 ounces) tomato sauce
    1 package taco seasoning mix (about 1½ ounces)
    2 cups green or red bell pepper strips
 1½ cups corn, fresh or frozen
    2 cups quick-cooking rice, white or brown
       Grated cheese (optional)
       Sliced ripe olives (optional)
       Crushed tortilla chips (optional)

Heat oil over medium-high heat in large skillet. Add garlic and lamb strips. Cook and stir until lamb is no longer pink. Add broth, tomato sauce and seasoning mix. Bring to a boil; reduce heat. Cover and simmer 5 minutes. Add bell peppers and corn. Bring to a boil; stir in rice. Remove from heat. Cover and let stand 5 minutes or until moisture is absorbed. Fluff with fork. Serve with grated cheese, sliced ripe olives and crushed tortilla chips, if desired.

Makes 6 servings

*Favorite recipe from **American Lamb Council***

Nutrients per Serving: Calories: 331 (27% of Calories from Fat), Total Fat: 10 g, Saturated Fat: 3 g, Cholesterol: 69 mg, Protein: 26 g, Carbohydrate: 34 g, Sodium: 539 mg, Fiber: 2 g

Cheesy Polenta with Zucchini Stew

2¼ cups water, divided
1 cup stone-ground or regular yellow cornmeal
2 eggs
2 egg whites
¾ cup (3 ounces) reduced-fat sharp Cheddar cheese
1 jalapeño pepper,* minced
1 teaspoon margarine
½ teaspoon salt, divided
1 tablespoon olive oil
1 cup chopped onion
2 cups coarsely chopped peeled eggplant
3 cloves minced garlic
3 cups chopped zucchini
1 cup chopped tomato
½ cup chopped yellow bell pepper
2 tablespoons minced fresh parsley
1 tablespoon minced fresh oregano
¼ teaspoon minced fresh rosemary
¼ teaspoon ground pepper blend

*Jalapeño peppers can sting and irritate the skin; wear rubber gloves when handling peppers and do not touch eyes. Wash hands after handling peppers.

1. Bring 2 cups water to a boil. Slowly add cornmeal, stirring constantly. Bring to a boil, stirring constantly, until mixture thickens. Lightly beat eggs and egg whites with remaining ¼ cup water. Add to cornmeal; cook and stir until bubbly. Remove from heat; stir in cheese, jalapeño pepper, margarine and ¼ teaspoon salt. Pour into 9-inch square baking pan. Cover and refrigerate several hours or until firm.

2. Heat oil in medium saucepan over medium heat until hot. Cook and stir onion, eggplant and garlic 5 minutes or until onion is transparent. Add zucchini, tomato, bell pepper, parsley, oregano, rosemary, remaining ¼ teaspoon salt and pepper blend. Simmer, uncovered, 1 hour.

3. Spray large nonstick skillet with nonstick vegetable cooking spray. Heat skillet over medium heat until hot. Cut polenta in 6 rectangles. Cook over medium heat 8 minutes on each side or until crusty and lightly browned. Serve zucchini stew over polenta. *Makes 6 servings*

Nutrients per Serving: Calories: 219 (30% of Calories from Fat), Total Fat: 7 g, Saturated Fat: 2 g, Cholesterol: 79 mg, Protein: 10 g, Carbohydrate: 29 g, Sodium: 437 mg, Fiber: 3 g

351

Ravioli with Homemade Tomato Sauce

3 cloves garlic, peeled
½ cup fresh basil leaves
3 cups seeded, peeled tomatoes, cut into quarters
2 tablespoons tomato paste
2 tablespoons fat-free Italian salad dressing
1 tablespoon balsamic vinegar
¼ teaspoon black pepper
1 package (9 ounces) refrigerated reduced-fat cheese ravioli
2 cups shredded spinach leaves
1 cup (4 ounces) shredded part-skim mozzarella cheese

MICROWAVE DIRECTIONS

1. To prepare tomato sauce, process garlic in food processor until coarsely chopped. Add basil; process until coarsely chopped. Add tomatoes, tomato paste, salad dressing, vinegar and pepper; process using on/off pulsing action until tomatoes are chopped.

2. Spray 9-inch square microwavable dish with nonstick cooking spray. Spread 1 cup tomato sauce in dish. Layer half of ravioli and spinach over tomato sauce. Repeat layers with 1 cup tomato sauce and remaining ravioli and spinach. Top with remaining 1 cup of tomato sauce.

3. Cover with plastic wrap; refrigerate 1 to 8 hours. Vent plastic wrap. Microwave at MEDIUM (50%) 20 minutes or until pasta is tender and hot. Sprinkle with cheese. Microwave at HIGH 3 minutes or just until cheese melts. Let stand, covered, 5 minutes before serving.

Makes 6 servings

Nutrients per Serving: Calories: 206 (26% of Calories from Fat), Total Fat: 6 g, Saturated Fat: 3 g, Cholesterol: 40 mg, Protein: 13 g, Carbohydrate: 26 g, Sodium: 401 mg, Fiber: 3 g

Ravioli with Homemade Tomato Sauce

Tuna Noodle Casserole

6 ounces uncooked noodles
1 tablespoon margarine
8 ounces fresh mushrooms, sliced
1 small onion, chopped
1 cup fat-free reduced-sodium chicken broth
1 cup fat-free (skim) milk
¼ cup all-purpose flour
1 can (12¼ ounces) tuna packed in water, drained
1 cup frozen peas, thawed
1 jar (2 ounces) chopped pimiento, drained
½ teaspoon dried thyme leaves
¼ teaspoon salt
⅛ teaspoon black pepper

1. Cook noodles according to package directions, omitting salt. Drain; cover. Set aside.

2. Meanwhile, melt margarine in large nonstick skillet over medium-high heat. Add mushrooms and onion; cook and stir 5 minutes or until onion is tender.

3. Using wire whisk, blend chicken broth, milk and flour in small bowl. Stir into mushroom mixture; bring to a boil. Cook and stir about 2 minutes or until thickened. Reduce heat to medium; stir in tuna, peas, pimiento, thyme and salt. Add noodles and pepper; mix thoroughly.

4. Preheat oven to 350°F. Spray 2-quart casserole with nonstick cooking spray. Spread noodle mixture evenly in prepared casserole. Bake 30 minutes or until bubbly and heated through. Let stand 5 minutes before serving.

Makes 6 servings

Nutrients per Serving: Calories: 254 (11% of Calories from Fat), Total Fat: 3 g, Saturated Fat: 1 g, Cholesterol: 18 mg, Protein: 23 g, Carbohydrate: 33 g, Sodium: 585 mg, Fiber: 2 g

Boca® Pasta Bake

1 box (12 ounces) frozen BOCA® Crumbles
8 ounces mostaccioli, cooked and drained
1 jar (28 to 30 ounces) spaghetti sauce
¾ cup KRAFT® Reduced Fat Parmesan Style Grated Topping, divided
1 package (8 ounces) KRAFT® 2% Milk Shredded Reduced Fat Mozzarella Cheese

HEAT oven to 375°F. Spray 13×9-inch baking dish with no stick cooking spray.

MIX crumbles, pasta, spaghetti sauce and ½ cup Parmesan topping.

SPOON into prepared dish. Top with mozzarella cheese; sprinkle with remaining ¼ cup Parmesan topping.

BAKE 25 to 30 minutes.

Makes 8 servings

Prep Time: 15 minutes
Bake Time: 30 minutes

Nutrients per Serving: Calories: 430 (27% of Calories from Fat), Total Fat: 13 g, Saturated Fat: 5 g, Cholesterol: 25 mg, Protein: 26 g, Carbohydrate: 52 g, Sodium: 1310 mg, Fiber: 7 g

Add 1 box (10 ounces) chopped frozen spinach, thawed and well drained, to the crumbles mixture before spooning into baking dish.

Broccoli & Potato Chowder

1 can (about 14 ounces) fat-free, reduced-sodium chicken broth
1 cup sliced leeks
1 medium peeled potato, cubed
⅓ cup fresh or frozen corn
1 can (about 4 ounces) mild green chilies
¾ teaspoon paprika
1½ cups broccoli florets
¾ cup evaporated skimmed milk
2 tablespoons all-purpose flour
Jalapeño pepper sauce (optional)

1. In medium saucepan combine broth, leeks, potato, corn, chilies and paprika. Bring to a boil. Reduce heat and simmer, covered, 10 to 15 minutes or until vegetables are tender. Add broccoli; simmer 3 minutes.

2. Whisk milk into flour. Stir into vegetable mixture. Cook, stirring constantly, until soup comes to a boil and thickens slightly. Season to taste with pepper sauce, if desired.

Makes 2 servings

357

Nutrients per Serving: **Calories:** 280 (3% of Calories from Fat), **Total Fat:** 1 g, **Saturated Fat:** <1 g, **Cholesterol:** 3 mg, **Protein:** 19 g, **Carbohydrate:** 51 g, **Sodium:** 311 mg, **Fiber:** 5 g

Helpful Hint

Evaporated skimmed milk, which has 60% of its water removed, contributes richness without fat to soups and sauces when it is used undiluted. If you don't like its flavor, you may substitute fat-free (skim) milk.

Spinach and Mushroom Enchiladas

2 packages (10 ounces each) frozen chopped spinach, thawed
1½ cups sliced mushrooms
1 can (15 ounces) pinto beans, drained and rinsed
3 teaspoons chili powder, divided
¼ teaspoon red pepper flakes
1 can (8 ounces) reduced-sodium tomato sauce
2 tablespoons water
½ teaspoon hot pepper sauce
8 (8-inch) corn tortillas
1 cup (4 ounces) shredded Monterey Jack cheese
Shredded lettuce (optional)
Chopped tomatoes (optional)
Reduced-fat sour cream (optional)

1. Combine spinach, mushrooms, beans, 2 teaspoons chili powder and red pepper flakes in large skillet over medium heat. Cook and stir 5 minutes; remove from heat.

2. Combine tomato sauce, water, remaining 1 teaspoon chili powder and pepper sauce in medium skillet. Dip tortillas into tomato sauce mixture; stack tortillas on waxed paper.

3. Divide spinach filling into 8 portions. Spoon onto center of tortillas; roll up and place in 11×8-inch microwavable dish. (Secure rolls with wooden picks, if desired.) Spread remaining tomato sauce mixture over enchiladas.

4. Cover with vented plastic wrap. Microwave, uncovered, at MEDIUM (50%) 10 minutes or until heated through. Sprinkle with cheese. Microwave at MEDIUM 3 minutes or until cheese is melted. Serve with lettuce, tomatoes and sour cream, if desired. *Makes 4 servings*

Nutrients per Serving: Calories: 371 (26% of Calories from Fat), Total Fat: 11 g, Saturated Fat: 6 g, Cholesterol: 25 mg, Protein: 20 g, Carbohydrate: 52 g, Sodium: 666 mg, Fiber: 12 g

Double Corn & Cheddar Chowder

        1 tablespoon margarine
        1 cup chopped onion
        2 tablespoons all-purpose flour
     2½ cups fat-free reduced-sodium chicken broth
        1 can (16 ounces) cream-style corn
        1 cup frozen whole kernel corn
       ½ cup finely diced red bell pepper
       ½ teaspoon hot pepper sauce
       ¾ cup (3 ounces) shredded sharp Cheddar cheese
          Black pepper (optional)

1. Melt margarine in large saucepan over medium heat. Add onion; cook and stir 5 minutes. Sprinkle onion with flour; cook and stir 1 minute.

2. Add chicken broth; bring to a boil, stirring frequently. Add cream-style corn, corn kernels, bell pepper and pepper sauce; bring to a simmer. Cover; simmer 15 minutes.

3. Remove from heat; gradually stir in cheese until melted. Ladle into soup bowls; sprinkle with black pepper, if desired.

Makes 6 servings

Nutrients per Serving: Calories: 180 (28% of Calories from Fat), Total Fat: 6 g, Saturated Fat: 2 g, Cholesterol: 10 mg, Protein: 7 g, Carbohydrate: 28 g, Sodium: 498 mg, Fiber: 2 g

Helpful Hint

Since cheese is high in fat it is important to limit the amount used in light recipes. Sharp Cheddar cheese has more flavor per ounce than its mild counterpart, so you can use less. You may substitute reduced-fat sharp Cheddar cheese and reduce the fat grams per serving even more.

360

Double Corn & Cheddar Chowder

Spinach Lasagna

1 container (16 ounces) BREAKSTONES® or KNUDSEN'S® 2% Cottage Cheese
1 package (10 ounces) frozen chopped spinach, thawed, well drained
2 cups KRAFT® Shredded Low-Moisture Part Skim Mozzarella Cheese, divided
½ cup KRAFT® Reduced Fat Parmesan Style Grated Topping, divided
1 egg, beaten
1 jar (28 ounces) spaghetti sauce, divided
6 lasagna noodles, cooked, drained

HEAT oven to 350°F.

MIX cottage cheese, spinach, 1 cup of the mozzarella cheese, ¼ cup of the grated topping and egg.

LAYER 1 cup of the spaghetti sauce, ½ of the lasagna noodles and ½ of the cottage cheese mixture in 13×9-inch baking dish. Repeat layers, ending with sauce. Sprinkle remaining 1 cup mozzarella cheese and ¼ cup of the grated topping.

BAKE 45 minutes. Let stand 10 minutes before serving.   *Makes 10 servings*

Prep Time: 25 minutes
Bake Time: 45 minutes plus standing

Nutrients per Serving: Calories: 280 (35% of Calories from Fat), Total Fat: 11 g, Saturated Fat: 4.5 g, Cholesterol: 45 mg, Protein: 16 g, Carbohydrate: 30 g, Sodium: 890 mg, Fiber: 4 g

362

Easy Italian Vegetable Pasta Bake

3 cups mostaccioli, cooked, drained
1 jar (27½ ounces) light pasta sauce
1 package (8 ounces) KRAFT® 2% Milk Shredded Reduced Fat Mozzarella Cheese, divided
2 cups thinly sliced mushrooms
2 cups sliced halved yellow squash
2 cups sliced halved zucchini

MIX mostaccioli, pasta sauce, 1 cup of the cheese and vegetables in large bowl.

SPOON into 13×9-inch baking dish. Top with remaining cheese.

BAKE at 375°F for 20 to 25 minutes or until thoroughly heated.   *Makes 6 servings*

Prep Time: 15 minutes
Bake Time: 25 minutes

Nutrients per Serving: Calories: 370 (17% of Calories from Fat), Total Fat: 7 g, Saturated Fat: 4 g, Cholesterol: 20 mg, Protein: 21 g, Carbohydrate: 56 g, Sodium: 690 mg, Fiber: 6 g

Cheddar Cheese Strata

> 1 pound French bread, cut into ½- to ¾-inch slices, crusts removed, divided
> 2 cups (8 ounces) shredded reduced-fat Cheddar cheese, divided
> 2 whole eggs
> 3 egg whites
> 4 cups fat-free (skim) milk
> 1 teaspoon dry mustard
> 1 teaspoon grated fresh onion
> ½ teaspoon salt
>   Paprika to taste

1. Spray 13×9-inch glass baking dish with nonstick cooking spray. Place half the bread slices in bottom of prepared dish, overlapping slightly if necessary. Sprinkle with 1¼ cups cheese. Place remaining bread slices on top of cheese.

2. Whisk whole eggs and egg whites in large bowl. Add milk, mustard, onion and salt; whisk until well blended. Pour evenly over bread and cheese. Cover with remaining ¾ cup cheese and sprinkle with paprika. Cover and refrigerate 1 hour or overnight.

3. Preheat oven to 350°F. Bake about 45 minutes or until cheese is melted and bread is golden brown. Let stand 5 minutes before serving. Garnish with red bell pepper stars and fresh Italian parsley, if desired.   *Makes 8 servings*

Nutrients per Serving: Calories: 297 (23% of Calories from Fat), Total Fat: 7 g, Saturated Fat: 3 g, Cholesterol: 70 mg, Protein: 18 g, Carbohydrate: 38 g, Sodium: 962 mg, Fiber: <1 g

Stuffed Shells Florentine

1 cup (about 4 ounces) coarsely chopped mushrooms
½ cup chopped onion
1 clove garlic, minced
1 teaspoon Italian seasoning
¼ teaspoon ground black pepper
1 tablespoon FLEISCHMANN'S® Original Margarine
1 (16-ounce) container fat-free cottage cheese
1 (10-ounce) package frozen chopped spinach, thawed and well drained
½ cup EGG BEATERS® Healthy Real Egg Product
24 jumbo pasta shells, cooked in unsalted water and drained
1 (15¼-ounce) jar reduced-sodium spaghetti sauce

In large skillet, over medium-high heat, sauté mushrooms, onion, garlic, Italian seasoning and pepper in margarine until tender. Remove from heat; stir in cottage cheese, spinach and Egg Beaters®. Spoon mixture into shells.

Spread ½ cup spaghetti sauce in bottom of 13×9×2-inch baking dish; arrange shells over sauce. Top with remaining sauce; cover. Bake at 350°F for 35 minutes or until hot.

Makes 7 servings

Prep Time: 30 minutes
Cook Time: 40 minutes

Nutrients per Serving: Calories: 255 (7% of Calories from Fat), Total Fat: 2 g, Saturated Fat: 1 g, Cholesterol: 6 mg, Protein: 15 g, Carbohydrate: 35 g, Sodium: 515 mg, Fiber: 3 g

Vegetarian Chili

1 tablespoon vegetable oil
2 cloves garlic, finely chopped
1½ cups thinly sliced mushrooms
⅔ cup chopped red onion
⅔ cup chopped red bell pepper
2 teaspoons chili powder
¼ teaspoon ground cumin
⅛ teaspoon ground red pepper (optional)
⅛ teaspoon dried oregano leaves
1 can (28 ounces) peeled whole tomatoes
⅔ cup frozen baby lima beans
½ cup rinsed, drained canned Great Northern beans
4 tablespoons nonfat sour cream
4 tablespoons shredded reduced-fat Cheddar cheese

1. Heat oil in large nonstick saucepan over medium-high heat until hot. Add garlic. Cook and stir 3 minutes. Add mushrooms, onion and bell pepper. Cook 5 minutes, stirring occasionally. Add chili powder, cumin, red pepper, if desired, and oregano. Cook and stir 1 minute. Add tomatoes and beans. Reduce heat to medium-low. Simmer 15 minutes, stirring occasionally.

2. Serve with sour cream and cheese.   *Makes 4 servings*

Nutrients per Serving: Calories: 189 (24% of Calories from Fat), Total Fat: 5 g, Saturated Fat: 1 g, Cholesterol: 3 mg, Protein: 10 g, Carbohydrate: 29 g, Sodium: 428 mg, Fiber: 7 g

Tomato, Potato and Basil Skillet

1 tablespoon olive oil, divided
3 cups sliced potatoes
⅓ cup minced fresh basil
2 whole eggs
2 egg whites
2 tablespoons skim milk
1 tablespoon Dijon mustard
1 teaspoon dry mustard
½ teaspoon salt
¼ teaspoon black pepper
2 cups sliced plum tomatoes

1. Heat 1½ teaspoons oil in medium nonstick skillet over medium heat until hot. Layer half of potato slices in skillet. Cover and cook 3 minutes or until lightly browned. Turn potatoes and cook, covered, 3 minutes or until lightly browned. Remove potatoes from skillet. Repeat with remaining 1½ teaspoons oil and potatoes.

2. Arrange all potatoes in skillet. Sprinkle with basil. Whisk together eggs, egg whites, milk, mustards, salt and pepper in small bowl. Pour over potatoes. Arrange tomatoes over potato mixture. Reduce heat to low. Cover and cook 10 minutes or until eggs are set.

Makes 4 servings

Nutrients per Serving: Calories: 260 (23% of Calories from Fat), Total Fat: 7 g, Saturated Fat: 1 g, Cholesterol: 106 mg, Protein: 9 g, Carbohydrate: 42 g, Sodium: 394 mg, Fiber: 4 g

Lentil Stew over Couscous

1 large onion, chopped
1 green bell pepper, chopped
4 ribs celery, chopped
1 medium carrot, cut lengthwise into halves, then cut into 1-inch pieces
2 cloves garlic, chopped
3 cups lentils (1 pound), rinsed
1 can (14½ ounces) diced tomatoes, undrained
1 can (14½ ounces) reduced-sodium chicken broth
3 cups water
¼ teaspoon black pepper
1 teaspoon dried marjoram leaves
1 tablespoon cider vinegar
1 tablespoon olive oil
4½ to 5 cups hot cooked couscous
    Carrot curls (optional)
    Celery leaves (optional)

SLOW COOKER DIRECTIONS
Combine onion, bell pepper, celery, carrot, garlic, lentils, tomatoes with juice, broth, water, black pepper and marjoram in slow cooker. Stir; cover and cook on LOW 8 to 9 hours or until vegetables are tender.

Stir in vinegar and olive oil. Serve over couscous. Garnish with carrot curls and celery leaves, if desired.   *Makes 12 servings*

Tip: Lentil stew keeps well in the refrigerator for up to one week. Stew can also be frozen in airtight container in freezer up to three months.

Nutrients per Serving: Calories: 203 (9% of Calories from Fat), Total Fat: 2 g, Saturated Fat: <1 g, Cholesterol: 0 mg, Protein: 11 g, Carbohydrate: 37 g, Sodium: 128 mg, Fiber: 4 g

Cheesy Baked Barley

        2 cups water
    ½ cup medium pearled barley
    ½ teaspoon salt, divided
        Nonstick cooking spray
    ½ cup diced onion
    ½ cup diced zucchini
    ½ cup diced red bell pepper
    1½ teaspoons all-purpose flour
        Seasoned pepper
    ¾ cup fat-free (skim) milk
        1 cup (4 ounces) shredded reduced-fat Italian blend cheese, divided
        1 tablespoon Dijon mustard

1. Bring water to a boil in 1-quart saucepan. Add barley and ¼ teaspoon salt. Cover; reduce heat and simmer 45 minutes or until barley is tender and most of the water is evaporated. Let stand covered, 5 minutes.

2. Preheat oven to 375°F. Spray medium skillet with cooking spray. Cook onion, zucchini and bell pepper over medium-low heat about 10 minutes or until soft. Stir in flour, remaining ¼ teaspoon salt and seasoned pepper to taste; cook 1 to 2 minutes. Add milk, stirring constantly; cook and stir until slightly thickened. Remove from heat and add barley, ¾ cup cheese and mustard; stir until cheese is melted.

3. Spread in even layer in casserole. Sprinkle with remaining ¼ cup cheese. Bake 20 minutes or until hot. Preheat broiler. Broil casserole 1 to 2 minutes or until cheese is lightly browned.

Makes 2 servings

Nutrients per Serving: Calories: 362 (23% of Calories from Fat), Total Fat: 9 g, Saturated Fat: 4 g, Cholesterol: 32 mg, Protein: 20 g, Carbohydrate: 50 g, Sodium: 1159 mg, Fiber: 6 g

Cheesy Baked Barley

Acknowledgements

The publisher would like to thank the companies and organizations listed below for the use of their recipes and photographs in this publication.

A.1.® Steak Sauce
American Lamb Council
Barilla America, Inc.
Birds Eye®
Bob Evans®
Butterball® Turkey Company
ConAgra Foods®
Cucina Classica Italiana, Inc.
Del Monte Corporation
Delmarva Poultry Industry, Inc.
Egg Beaters®
The Golden Grain Company®
Hebrew National®
Heinz U.S.A.
The Hidden Valley® Food Products Company
Holland House® is a registered trademark of Mott's, Inc.
Hormel Foods, LLC
Kahlúa® Liqueur
Kraft Foods Holdings
Lawry's® Foods, Inc.
McCormick®
McIlhenny Company (TABASCO® brand Pepper Sauce)
National Chicken Council / US Poultry & Egg Association
National Pork Board
National Turkey Federation
Nestlé USA
Newman's Own, Inc.®
Norseland, Inc. / Lucini Italia Co.
Perdue Farms Incorporated
Reckitt Benckiser Inc.
Riviana Foods Inc.
The J.M. Smucker Company
StarKist® Seafood Company
Tyson Foods, Inc.
Uncle Ben's Inc.
Unilever Bestfoods North America
USA Rice Federation
Veg•All®
Wisconsin Milk Marketing Board

372

373

383

METRIC CONVERSION CHART

VOLUME MEASUREMENTS (dry)

1/8 teaspoon = 0.5 mL
1/4 teaspoon = 1 mL
1/2 teaspoon = 2 mL
3/4 teaspoon = 4 mL
1 teaspoon = 5 mL
1 tablespoon = 15 mL
2 tablespoons = 30 mL
1/4 cup = 60 mL
1/3 cup = 75 mL
1/2 cup = 125 mL
2/3 cup = 150 mL
3/4 cup = 175 mL
1 cup = 250 mL
2 cups = 1 pint = 500 mL
3 cups = 750 mL
4 cups = 1 quart = 1 L

VOLUME MEASUREMENTS (fluid)

1 fluid ounce (2 tablespoons) = 30 mL
4 fluid ounces (1/2 cup) = 125 mL
8 fluid ounces (1 cup) = 250 mL
12 fluid ounces (1 1/2 cups) = 375 mL
16 fluid ounces (2 cups) = 500 mL

WEIGHTS (mass)

1/2 ounce = 15 g
1 ounce = 30 g
3 ounces = 90 g
4 ounces = 120 g
8 ounces = 225 g
10 ounces = 285 g
12 ounces = 360 g
16 ounces = 1 pound = 450 g

DIMENSIONS

1/16 inch = 2 mm
1/8 inch = 3 mm
1/4 inch = 6 mm
1/2 inch = 1.5 cm
3/4 inch = 2 cm
1 inch = 2.5 cm

OVEN TEMPERATURES

250°F = 120°C
275°F = 140°C
300°F = 150°C
325°F = 160°C
350°F = 180°C
375°F = 190°C
400°F = 200°C
425°F = 220°C
450°F = 230°C

BAKING PAN SIZES

Utensil	Size in Inches/Quarts	Metric Volume	Size in Centimeters
Baking or Cake Pan (square or rectangular)	8×8×2	2 L	20×20×5
	9×9×2	2.5 L	23×23×5
	12×8×2	3 L	30×20×5
	13×9×2	3.5 L	33×23×5
Loaf Pan	8×4×3	1.5 L	20×10×7
	9×5×3	2 L	23×13×7
Round Layer Cake Pan	8×1½	1.2 L	20×4
	9×1½	1.5 L	23×4
Pie Plate	8×1¼	750 mL	20×3
	9×1¼	1 L	23×3
Baking Dish or Casserole	1 quart	1 L	—
	1½ quart	1.5 L	—
	2 quart	2 L	—